PITCAIRN

Richard Bean

PITCAIRN

OBERON BOOKS
LONDON

WWW.OBERONBOOKS.COM

First published in 2014 by Oberon Books Ltd
521 Caledonian Road, London N7 9RH
Tel: +44 (0) 20 7607 3637 / Fax: +44 (0) 20 7607 3629
e–mail: info@oberonbooks.com
www.oberonbooks.com

A catalogue record for this book is available from the British
Library.

PB ISBN: 978-1-78319-107-9
E ISBN: 978-1-78319-606-7

Cover design is by SWD swd.uk.com

Printed, bound and converted
by CPI Group (UK) Ltd, Croydon, CR0 4YY.

Visit www.oberonbooks.com to read more about all our books
and to buy them. You will also find features, author interviews and
news of any author events, and you can sign up for e–newsletters
so that you're always first to hear about our new releases.

"The mighty Out of Joint"
Time Out

"Inventive, individual and humane"
Whatsonstage.com

Inquisitive, epic, authentic and original: Out of Joint is a national and international touring theatre company, developing entertaining theatre that broadens horizons and investigates our times.

For 20 years, under the direction of Max Stafford-Clark, Out of Joint has premiered plays from leading writers including April De Angelis, Sebastian Barry, Richard Bean, Alistair Beaton, Caryl Churchill, David Hare, Robin Soans and Timberlake Wertenbaker, as well as launching the careers of writers such as Mark Ravenhill and Stella Feehily.

Out of Joint co-produces with the country's most exiting theatres. It has performed at the National Theatre and Royal Court, and its work has been seen in six continents - its recent revival of *Our Country's Good* tours overseas in 2014, and plays Richmond, Brighton and Windsor in November. Back home, Out of Joint also pursues an extensive education programme, which recently explanded to include not only work with education establishments but also writing and devising courses for participants of all ages.

Out of Joint
7 Thane Works, London N7 7NU
Tel: 020 7609 0207
Email: ojo@outofjoint.co.uk
Web: www.outofjoint.co.uk

Director: **Max Stafford-Clark**
Producer: **Panda Cox**
Associate Producer: **Graham Cowley**
Marketing Manager: **Jon Bradfield**
Company Administrator: **Martin Derbyshire**
PA & Education Administrator: **Isabel Quinzaños**
Finance Officer: **Sandra Rapley**

EDUCATION

Out of Joint offers a diverse programme of workshops and discussions for groups coming to see our performances, as well writing courses and resource packs.

Since 2012, Out of Joint has run an **Associate University Programme** to build and strengthen our relationship with universities by providing opportunities to collaborate, learn and develop new work. For instance, research and development work with Hertfordshire University led to the development of a new Rebecca Lenkiewicz play about witch trials in rural Hertfordshire, which will be toured nationally by Out of Joint.

The programme offers participating institutions two workshops (one with Max Stafford-Clark) and a weeklong mentoring internship at Out of Joint. Current Associate Universities are the universities of Essex Hertfordshire, Hull, Lincoln and Warwick, and Trinity College Dublin.

If you are interested in Out of Joint's education offering, including the Associate University Programme, please contact Isabel Quinzaños our Education Administrator.

Out of Joint is a Registered Charity No. 1033059

LOTTERY FUNDED

Supported using public funding by

ARTS COUNCIL ENGLAND

KEEP IN TOUCH
For information on our shows, tour details and offers, get in touch as above, or join our mailing list via our website. We are also on Twitter and Facebook.

THANK YOU
Out of Joint is hugely grateful to the generous people whose support is increasingly vital in enabling us to make and tour ambitious theatre. If you would like to give to Out of Joint - and perhaps get involved by supporting specific projects - call us on 020 7609 0207 or email Martin@outofjoint.co.uk. *Our heartfelt thanks to:*

Anonymous
Kate Ashfield
The Baring Foundation
Linda Bassett
Richard Bean
Alistair Beaton
John Blackmore
Danny Boyle
Frank & Elizabeth Brenan
David Brooks
Anthony Burton
Rachel Chambers
Guy Chapman
Chipo Chung
The David Cohen Charitable Trust
The John S Cohen Foundation
Jeremy Conway

Ron Cook
Dominic Cooke
Peter & Angela Cox
Eastwell Manor
Elyse Dodgson
The Eranda Foundation
John Lewis Partnership
Josephine Fenton
Roy Foster
The Foundation for Sport and the Arts
Friends of Theatre
Iain Gillie
Richard & Mary Gillie
The Granada Foundation
Edwina Grosvenor
The Paul Hamlyn Foundation
Mr & Mrs Harter

Andy Herrity
Harold Hyam Wingate Foundation
Kenneth Houston
Roland Jaquarello
Paul Jesson
James Jones
Mary Kerr & Roger Boden
Lord Kinnock
Rebecca Lenkiewicz
Michael & Jill Lewis
Philida Lloyd
Cameron Mackintosh
Amanda Mccleary
Ian McKellan
Juliet Meinrath
The Olivier Foundation
Ali Ostrer
David Owen Norris

The Prudential Awards
The Peggy Ramsay Foundation
Ian Redford
Alan Rickman
David Rintoul
Royal Victoria Hall Foundation
Max Stafford-Clark
Tom Stoppard
Trudie Styler
Karl Sydow
Ripley Talbot
Unity Theatre Trust
Richard Wilson
Yorkshire Bank Charitable Trust

ONLINE BOOKSHOP
Visit Out of Joint's online shop to buy play scripts and theatre books at discounted prices: www.outofjoint.co.uk

Photos: Opposite page: Top Girls by Caryl Churchill in rehearsal, photo by Manuel Harlan; The Queen and I by Sue Townsend and The Big Fellah by Richard Bean, photos by John Haynes. Previous page Bang Bang Bang by Stella Feehily, photo by John Haynes.

CHICHESTER FESTIVAL THEATRE

Chichester Festival Theatre is one of the UK's flagship theatres with an international reputation for producing work of the highest quality, ranging from large-scale musicals to distinguished dramas.

Festival 2014 is a landmark season for Chichester. It marks the reopening of the newly refurbished Chichester Festival Theatre following a major capital project, RENEW, to restore and upgrade its Grade 2* listed building. Chichester Festival Theatre can now proudly match its world-class artistic reputation with world-class spaces. The Festival Theatre reopened in July with a major production of Peter Shaffer's *Amadeus* directed by Jonathan Church with Rupert Everett as Salieri. The season also includes two award-winning Broadway musicals (*Guys and Dolls*, *Gypsy*), three world premieres which reveal hidden stories behind historical events (*Pressure*, *Pitcairn*, *Taken at Midnight*) and compelling drama (*Stevie*, *Frankie & Johnny* in the *Clair de Lune*, *Miss Julie*, *Black Comedy*, *An Ideal Husband*).

During 2014, Chichester Festival Theatre productions will continue to be seen by the widest possible audience beyond West Sussex. *Singin' in the Rain* continues its UK tour until October 2014 and *Barnum* begins a UK tour in the autumn. *The Pajama Game* is at the Shaftesbury Theatre in the West End for a limited season and *Another Country* is on tour following a run at Trafalgar Studios. *The Last Confession*, directed by Jonathan Church, tours to Canada, America and Australia. *Private Lives* was recently broadcast at cinemas throughout the UK.

In 2013, the theatre's West End transfers included *The Resistible Rise of Arturo Ui*, *Singin' in the Rain*, *Private Lives*, *Kiss Me, Kate* and the Oliver Award-winning production *Goodnight Mister Tom*. The highly acclaimed production of *King Lear* with Frank Langella completed a limited New York run in February 2014.

Chairman **Sir William Castell**
Artistic Director **Jonathan Church**
Executive Director **Alan Finch**

cft.org.uk

Founded by the pioneering American actor and director Sam Wanamaker, Shakespeare's Globe is a unique international resource dedicated to the exploration of Shakespeare's work and the theatre for which he wrote. From modest beginnings, Shakespeare's Globe has become one of the most popular visitor destinations in the UK, at the heart of the regeneration of London's Bankside. Shakespeare's Globe is a UK registered charity and continues to operate without annual government funding.

Under the leadership of Artistic Director Dominic Dromgoole, the Globe Theatre has gained an international reputation for performance excellence, welcoming over one million visitors annually.

Pitcairn is one of four new plays to be staged in 2014, with *Doctor Scroggy's War* by Howard Brenton, *Holy Warriors* by David Eldridge and Simon Armitage's *The Last Days of Troy*.

Sam Wanamaker Playhouse
This year saw the completion of the new indoor Jacobean theatre, which opened with *The Duchess of Malfi* and which will continue to stage Jacobean dramas, new plays, opera and candlelit concerts.

Globe to Globe
The *Hamlet* tour opened at the Globe on 23 April 2014 – the 450th anniversary of Shakespeare's birth. Over the course of the two-year project, the company will travel to hundreds of unique, atmospheric venues across seven continents by boat, sleeper train, jeep, tall ship, bus and airplane. As part of the Globe's ongoing commitment to the international celebration of Shakespeare the Bankside theatre hosted *All's Well That Ends Well* in Gujarati in May, and *A Midsummer Night's Dream* in British Sign Language in June.

Globe Education
Each year, more than 100,000 people of all ages and nationalities participate in Globe Education's programme of public events, workshops and courses. Globe Education also runs an extensive programme in the Southwark community and creates national and international outreach projects for students and teachers.

Globe Exhibition & Tour
Open all year round, the Globe Exhibition & Tour provides an opportunity for all ages, families and groups to learn more about Shakespeare, his London and the theatre for which he wrote. Live demonstrations explore stage-fighting, Elizabethan clothing, and printing on a traditional press.

shakespearesglobe.com

UTOPIAS | by Tom Wicker

Taylor Camp, Kauai, Hawaii, by John Wehrheim. His book of photographs and interviews, *Taylor Camp*, is published by Serindia Contemporary; he has also produced a documentary of the same name.

Early on in Richard Bean's *Pitcairn*, Ned Young surveys the work of his fellow Bounty mutineer William Brown, who has been appointed the island's 'gardener'. Upon finding Brown, Young exclaims: "Look at this! William, you have turned the Garden of Eden into… Norwich."

It's a funny line, and seemingly glib, but neatly encapsulates the provinciality of even our grandest ideals. Whether it's British hedgerows or greed and desire, it can be hard to shake off the things we believe we have left behind – however far we travel.

But yet we keep searching for 'utopia' – a fairer, usually simpler place, free from the failings of whichever society has let us down. And throughout history, this quest has blended the literal with the metaphorical. When Bean has one character marvelling that "we find ourselves at the beginning of time," he's tapping into a longstanding tradition of locating paradise abroad.

From the earliest travel reports to Thomas More's hugely influential book of 1516, in which Utopia is an island, our notions of a better place have been anchored to the idea that it is somewhere else. Oscar Wilde once wrote that "a map of the world that does not include Utopia is not even worth glancing at, for it leaves out the one country at which Humanity is always landing."

Utopia as a place carved out far from civilisation is a pervasive idea throughout art and literature, glimpsed in everything from *The Swiss Family Robinson* to Alex Garland's *The Beach*. It's usually an unspoilt space – like somewhere from before The Fall, whether that's the Garden of Eden or pre-capitalism. It's about wiping the slate clean and starting again by getting back to nature.

Equating moral goodness with a return to life in a 'state of nature' gained huge traction in the eighteenth century. It was popularised by the French philosopher Jean Jacques Rousseau, who argued that the advent of modern society, with its focus on private ownership and self-advancement, had destroyed the natural bonds of community that provide true freedom.

But what we laud as a 'state of nature' is often just a sublimated version of our own values and principles disguised by pretty foliage. Bean makes this point with black humour in *Pitcairn*. Grand talk of "Man and Woman in a natural state," living "without prejudices" and "knowing no other god but love", is followed by utter incredulity at the notion that the island's females might receive equal property rights.

Religion has been central to real-life attempts to build new societies. It's pivotal to the narrative of modern-day Pitcairn's history and helped to propel The Mayflower into the New World more than a century before the mutiny on The Bounty. But utopia-like origin myths tend to sweep tricky truths beneath the carpet – for every celebratory Pilgrim Fathers story there are displaced Native Americans.

In Bean's take on Pitcairn, religion is a tool to be exploited. Talk of the will of God is used to subjugate others on the island after a revolt. In this sense, utopia and a repressive, Orwellian *1984*-style dystopia are not separate states – the latter is the dark side of the coin when an ideology is threatened or someone's survival is at stake. When disease or hunger strike, the rhetoric of harmony and equality tends to disappear.

In the end, it's all relative, however you dress it up. But the urge to create utopia is enduring. People continue to cleave to the idea that things will be better if they can recreate an imagined 'start' or an earlier time. This desire is particularly acute when times are tough – when we feel that an existing society has let us down, whether financially, politically or culturally.

In the increasingly secular western world of the past century, religion as the driving force for returning to an idealised origin point has been translated into nostalgia for a past in which everyone left their doors unlocked and neighbours helped each other out. One of the most literal manifestations of this is Celebration, the purpose-built town developed by the Walt Disney Company – pure Americana with white picket fences, piped music and even artificial snow-falls.

Barring one murder, Celebration has been praised for its safety. But many have found this picture-perfect idyll – which opened its gates in

1996 – unsettling. Its neatness and order seem inimical to real life. And the homogeneity of such master-planned communities, with their manifestoes and rules, can feel exclusionary. Perhaps unsurprisingly, a 2010 census revealed that 91% of Celebration's population was white.

A very different kind of utopia-building was Taylor Camp, on the Hawaiian island of Kauai. Started in 1969 by 13 hippies on land given to them by the brother of actress Elizabeth Taylor, it grew into a community that lasted for eight years. As detailed in John Wehrheim's absorbing eponymous photographic history of the camp, this complex of treehouses was filled by those who had rejected mainstream society's values.

Now, it would be easy to scoff at Taylor Camp's clothes-optional, flower-power set-up. The 'dippy-hippy' stereotype has had decades to take root. But the camp was a response to a time of huge social upheaval, as the fight for civil rights intensified and America reeled from the Vietnam War and then Watergate. It offered both a refuge and an alternative way of life to a deeply disillusioned younger generation.

Apart from a few troublemakers, life in Taylor Camp – which deliberately had no designated 'leader' – seems largely to have been harmonious. But, nevertheless, writes Wehrheim, it was seen by the indigenous islanders as a disruption of their lives. However well-intentioned they might have been, people weren't flooding into a conveniently deserted paradise. Kauai had its own customs and practices. And Taylor Camp only lasted as long as it did because of a resourceful local lawyer. For the majority of its existence, he succeeded in fending off attempts by the state Attorney General's office to evict the inhabitants. When the government finally won, state employees shipped out the remaining residents and torched the site. Since then, Kauai has become a tourist hotspot. There's a park where the camp used to be.

Real-life Utopias are fragile – vulnerable to the same vagaries of human nature and commercial imperatives as anything else. Even in its best years, Taylor Camp couldn't entirely shut out the rest of the world. The local shop accepted government food stamps; and while some campers owned businesses, others lived on state welfare. Cutting all ties with whichever society we are trying to leave behind is no easy task.

That was certainly the lesson of *Castaway*, the BBC's reality TV social experiment from 2000. The programme followed a group of men, women and children as they attempted to establish a self-sufficient, sustainable community on an isolated Scottish island. It was a classic example of the back-to-basics impulse; another attempt to return to a 'truer' state of nature.

But the problems that beset the group showed how enmeshed in the modern world they still were. A flu outbreak saw some shipped off the island, while a nearby case of meningitis prompted the programme-makers to supply everyone with antibiotics. And although the volunteers may have fallen short of actually killing each other, there is kinship between their jealousies, rivalries and cliques and the tensions of the settlers in *Pitcairn*.

If there is a connecting thread throughout all of this, it is people's tendency to treat the spaces in which they seek to carve out their utopias as little more than reflections of their dreams and ideals, rather than real places. Such ignorance can lead to disaster. Several of Pitcairn's early settlers were wiped out by disease, as were many Pilgrim Fathers before them. Countless grand social schemes have come crashing to the ground because of a fundamental lack of knowledge.

A recent case in point is the complete failure of Fordlândia, a now-abandoned industrial town erected deep in the Amazon Rainforest in 1928 by the industrialist Henry Ford, to secure a source of rubber for Ford Motor Company. His utopian vision of creating a model community in the jungles of Brazil quickly fell apart, as disgruntled native workers clashed with – and eventually revolted against – the US-style management of the factory, food and accommodation.

On top of this, Ford's managers didn't understand the complex tropical ecosystem of the Amazon. Rubber trees that had been widely spaced in the jungle were packed too closely together in plantations. These soon fell victim to tree blight and the depredations of countless insects – ultimately failing to produce the rubber that had been the point of Fordlândia in the first place.

This is the risk of seeking out utopia: while an idea may sound simple, people and places rarely are. And, too often, the successful realisation of one person's vision for society involves trampling another's into the dirt. But yet, it is built into our nature to keep departing for the next horizon – for better or for worse.

Tom Wicker is an arts writer and reviewer.

ON PITCAIRN | by Dea Birkett

Pitcairn | Wileypics/Flickr

When you leave the theatre tonight, or travel home, or go to work tomorrow morning, imagine this. That the first step of your journey is to clamber a rope ladder, lashing in the South Pacific winds above the ocean swells. Then you can begin to know what it is like to leave Pitcairn Island. This fist of volcanic rock, marooned in the South Pacific Ocean, is joined to the rest of the world by no more than this lashing rope ladder. With no natural harbour, the islanders take out a longboat to passing ships. The ship throws down a rope ladder and they ascend the steel cliff-high side to the deck. This ladder is the sole means of arrival and of escape.

The islanders – those of them hearty enough to man the longboats – leap for the rungs on the crest of a wave like pirates, making it look easy. But behind their effortless ability lies eight generations of sea trading. The descendants of mutineers, they first benefitted from, then have battled with this sea-bound isolation for over two centuries. Less than 50 of them remain on Pitcairn.

The Pitcairn story began at dawn on 28 April 1789, in the South Pacific off Tonga Island, when Fletcher Christian, Master's Mate of His Majesty's Armed Vessel Bounty, led a mutiny against Captain William Bligh. The Bounty was on a mission to collect breadfruit seedlings and transport them to the West Indies, to provide staple foodstuff for the slaves. But although Bligh was an outstanding navigator, having previously served under Captain James Cook, he was a poor commander, his stern, unforgiving manner losing the support of his men.

The Bounty had spent five months anchored off Tahiti as the breadfruit seedlings were gathered and grown. Here the crew lived on shore, had their buttocks tattooed Polynesian-style and shared their huts with local women. Returning to strict seaboard regime was like being cast back into a floating prison. The temptations of Tahiti still called them. Three weeks in to the return voyage, 24-year-old Christian rebelled, taking 25 of the crew with him.

Casting Bligh and his loyal followers adrift, the fugitives sailed back to Tahiti for women and food. Two thirds of the mutineers opted to stay, risking capture by the British. Just nine remained loyal to their new master, sailing off with 12 Tahitian women, six Polynesian men and one child. For nine months they dodged about the South Pacific, until stumbling across the tip of a volcano, mischarted by 200 miles, called Pitcairn Island. "Its beauty, its temperate climate and above all, in its now-demonstrated inaccessibility, Pitcairn was ideal," recorded one mutineer. The Bounty was burned, and the mutineers' one thread with the rest of humankind was cut. They disappeared from the face of the earth. For almost two decades, they were undiscovered. These are the years explored by Richard Bean's *Pitcairn*. When contact was finally made by an American whaler in 1808, only one mutineer remained – with ten women and 23 children.

Over the following century, Nantucket whalers, British merchant ships, French adventurers and naval vessels from Portsmouth called on the island, each describing the community as a perfect, pocket-sized community, close to Paradise. Born from mutiny, the Pitcairners continued to search out a new leader to free them from the infamy of their past. Messiahs washed up on the shore, promising to save the lonely flock, from the charismatic English adventurer George Hunn Nobbs to an American missionary called John Tay who arrived in 1886, clutching some Seventh Day Adventist literature. The whole island was converted and no other religion has been tolerated since.

The mutineers' newfound land is still the smallest and most remote country on earth. Put your finger in the middle of the big blue blanket that is the South Pacific, and it will land near Pitcairn, although it's too small to be marked. New Zealand is 3000 miles to the southwest, Tahiti 1300 miles to the northwest. The island covers under 1.75 square miles. There is no place you cannot hear the crash of the surf. The coast seethes with a white ruff of surf – cliffs and craggy rock faces battered by an untempered ocean. The only beach is Down Rope, called so because you have to climb down a rope nailed into a cliff face to reach it. It's here the only evidence of inhabitants before the mutineers exists – petroglyphs scratched onto the rock by early Polynesians, probably passing through a couple of centuries earlier. There was no reason to stay.

Approaching the island from the sea – the only way, as there is no airstrip – it looks little bigger than a ship. Passing ships may spot the white houses of Adamstown, the only settlement named after mutineer John Adams - faint among the banana trees and coconut palms. The houses are constructed from hardboard with tin roofs to catch the rain. From the ocean, you cannot see that many of them are abandoned.

Today's Pitcairn islanders, descendants of the mutineers and their Tahitian wives, are a bizarre hybrid race, some appearing thoroughly British, others Polynesian. They are huge, often obese, tall people with wide sprawled feet from walking barefoot. Overhearing a Pitcairn conversation is like listening to characters from the pages of Melville or Defoe. Guns are muskets, food is wekle (victuals) and to fall over is to capsize. It's a stew of 18th century English, Polynesian, modern obscenities picked up from passing sailors, and seafaring terms like all hands for everyone, and deck for floor. Even though they've been a British possession since 1839, and Pitcairn remains Britain's last overseas territory in the South Pacific, their tribal costume is T-Shirts and baseball caps sent by American wellwishers.

They spend their days fishing for nanwe (oily, bone-ridden flat fish) from the rocks or giant wahoo and shark from flat-bottomed wooden canoes, and farming. Orange, mango, plantain, grapefruit, avocado and banana trees flourish alongside the ubiquitous coconut. Fresh vegetables are grown in small family plots scattered all over the island. Tomatoes, cabbages, peas, sweet potatoes, cassava and beets can be planted year round. The earth is rampantly fertile - lettuce and beans sowed from seed are ready to eat within two months. There are annual harvests of arrowroot and sugar cane. Breadfruit – brought from the Bounty – are knocked from the trees with live bullets in their muskets.

Pitcairn's death knell has been sounded several times since its discovery in 1808. Two attempts were made to abandon the island – one to Tahiti in 1831, and another to Norfolk Island in 1856. Both failed, and the Pitcairners, diminished in number, returned to their rock. At its height, in the 1930s, the population was more than 230. But babies are few, and Pitcairn marriages are not made in heaven. Now there are just nine families, sharing four surnames – Christian, Young, Warren and Brown. The choice of mates is limited – you will have known them all your lives. Romantic love is not only rare, but in some aspects illegal. Local Pitcairn law forbids expressions of affection in public places.

When I was on the island, this yoke of conformity was felt keenly by the younger generation, who undertake their own mutiny by importing alcohol from the ships, smuggled ashore in plain brown bags. On Friday nights, the most sacred evening in the Adventist week, these rebels gathered to dance and drink. At the sound of the Tahitian song Waikiki Tamure, banished from the island for more than a century, they put down their cans of New Zealand beer and swing their hips to the seductive rhythm. It is as if a long-buried Polynesian cultural gene is rising.

Pitcairn lies on the Panama Canal to New Zealand shipping route, and vessels working that passage may pass within a few miles of the island. But there is no certainty when the next ship will call. There may be two in one month, then not another for four. When a ship is sighted offshore, the bell in the square rings five times and the whole island hurries down the unpaved Hill of Difficulty to the Landing. The men haul the longboat into Bounty Bay. The bay is no more than a dent in the iron-clad coastline, and provides no natural harbour. The 40-foot longboat is packed with people and goods for trade – fresh fruit, fish, baskets woven from pandanus, wooden carvings of the Bounty. (The islanders were taught to carve by an Austrian in 1920s and use a video of the 1935 Mutiny on the Bounty movie as the guide for their models, even though it no more resembles the real boat than Clark Gable accurately portrayed Fletcher Christian.)

Ten years ago, on the last day of August 2004, this familiar scene unfolded. The longboats aligned themselves against the side of the ship and a rope ladder was thrown down from the deck. The men scrambled on board and began to lower the cargo over the side, taking care in the pitching open sea. But among the regular goods – sacks of flour, drums of cooking oil, boxes of basic medical supplies, barrels of fuel – was a large consignment of high wire fencing and massive steel gates. The wire fencing and steel gates were for a new development on this remote outcrop. Pitcairn was building a prison.

Seven Pitcairners – almost two-thirds of the men on the island – were on trial for sexual offences ranging from gross indecency and indecent assault to rape. The accused - Jay Warren, Dennis Christian, Len Brown, Terry Young, Dave Brown, Steve Christian and Randy Christian - faced 96 charges between them. All were against children. (Jay Warren was acquitted.) Some argued that it was their hybrid Polynesian heritage that allowed them to have underage sex, even though there is no evidence that this was the case. Since then, more Pitcairners have been charged and found guilty. Four police officers are now permanently posted on the island. Pitcairn has become the most heavily policed community in the world.

The guilty men have to be let out of their newly-built prison to man the longboats when a ship calls, and clamber up the rope ladder. There wouldn't be enough capable men otherwise. As each ship raises their anchor for the world beyond, the islanders bid farewell from the longboat with a rousing sea shanty. Callers have reported hearing it for over a century. Strong voiced above the pounding swell, they sing the Goodbye Song. They wave to those high above on deck – 'We part but hope to meet again – goodbye, goodbye, goodbye.' At this last line, the ropes are cast off and the longboat turns towards Pitcairn, filled with a handful of fallible human beings, imprisoned by the ocean, bound by their past.

Dea Birkett is author of Serpent in Paradise, *about her time on Pitcairn Island.*

Out of Joint, Chichester Festival Theatre and Shakespeare's Globe present

PITCAIRN

a play by Richard Bean

Touring 2014

22 August – 20 September
Chichester Festival Theatre

22 September – 11 October
Shakespeare's Globe

14 – 18 October
Plymouth Theatre Royal

21 – 24 October
Warwick Arts Centre

28 October – 1 November
Yvonne Arnaud Theatre, Guildford

4 – 8 November
Devonshire Park Theatre, Eastbourne

11 – 15 November
Oxford Playhouse

18 – 22 November
Malvern Theatres

PRODUCTION CREDITS

Lois Chimimba	Te Lahu
Samuel Edward-Cook	Quintal
Vanessa Emme	Fasto
Eben Figueiredo	Hiti
Siubhan Harrison	Mi Mitti
Saffron Hocking	Te'o
Ash Hunter	Ned Young
Naveed	Khan Menalee
Cassie Layton	Mata
Anna Leong Brophy	Walua
Tom Morley	Fletcher Christian
Adam Newington	John Adams
Henry Pettigrew	William McKoy
David Rubin	Oha
Jack Tarlton	William Brown

Director **Max Stafford-Clark**
Designer **Tim Shortall**
Lighting Designer **Johanna Town**
Composer **Adam Pleeth**
Choreographer **Orian Michaeli**
Sound Designer **Emma Laxton**
Casting Director **Gabrielle Dawes CDG**
Associate Director **Tim Hoare**
Assistant Director **Jake Smith**

Production Manager **Sam Paterson**
Company Stage Manager **Sally Hughes**
Deputy Stage Manger **Rebecca James**
Assistant Stage Manager **Lou Ballard**
Costume Supervisor **Brigid Guy**
Props Supervisor **Celia Strainge**
Fight Director **Jonathan Waller**
Dialect Coach **Richard Ryder**
Re-lighter **Theo Chadha**
Set Construction **Set-Up Scenary**
Production Carpenter **Steve Bush**
Costume Makers **Alison Kirkpatrick, Karen Stott**
Mens costumes supplied by **Angels**
Wigs **Linda McKnight**
Tattoo Supervisor **Lorena Paton**
Production & rehearsal photography **Robert Workman**

Thanks to: Dea Birkett, Jeniffer Crothall and the National Maritime Museum, Rob Vinson. **Richard Bean would like to thank:** Max Stafford-Clark, Andy Michel and Dea Birkett.

THE COMPANY

LOIS CHIMIMBA | Te Lahu
Lois trained at Mountview. Theatre includes *Nightingale and Chase* (Albany Theatre), *A Long and Happy Life* (Vibrant Festival), *Laridae* (White Bear Theatre) and *Deep* (Talawa Theatre). Television includes *Holby City*. Film includes *Earth Air Fire Water*. Radio includes *The Three Musketeers*.

SAMUEL EDWARD-COOK | Quintal
Sam trained at RADA. Theatre includes *Titus Andronicus* (Shakespeare's Globe), *Our Big Land* (UK Tour), *King Lear* (Theatre Royal Bath), *Glory Dazed* (Edinburgh/ Adelaide/Soho Theatre) and *Boys* (Headlong/Nuffield/Hightide). Television includes *Peaky Blinders*, *Land Girls*, *Doctors*. Films include *Passenger* and *Magwitch*.

VANESSA EMME | Fasto
Vanessa trained at the Lir Academy Dublin, where productions included *Scenes from the Big Picture*, *Bold Girls*, *The Night Season*, *Into the Woods* and *Pains*

of Youth. Theatre includes *The Shadow of a Gunman* and *Stags and Hens* (The New Theatre, Dublin). Films include *The Anti Love Pill*, *Every Second Sunday*, *The Inside* and *Ghostwood*.

EBEN FIGUEIREDO | Hiti
Theatre includes *A Level Playing Field* (Workshop), *Courting Drama* (Theatre Renegade), *Pigeon English* (NYT/Bristol Old Vic), *Matt Smith Project*, *Social Inclusion Project*, *Olympic Team Welcoming Ceremony*, *Diana Bliss Tribute*, *Gold and Popcorn* and *Our Days of Rage* (all National Youth Theatre), *The Suit* (Young Vic) *East End Girls*, *Dream Girls* (Italia Conti), *The Ritual* (reading. National Theatre). He trained at Bristol Old Vic (graduated 2014) where shows included *The Promise*, *The Events*, *The School for Scandal* and *Othello*.

SIUBHAN HARRISON | Mi Mitti
Theatre includes *From Here To Eternity* (Shaftesbury Theatre), *Tommy* (Prince Edward Theatre), *The Soft of Her Palm, In Quest of Conscience* (Finborough Theatre), *Earthquakes in London* (Headlong Theatre Tour), *Grease* (Piccadilly Theatre), *Rich isn't Easy* (Tristan Bates Theatre), *The Stripper* (UK Tour), *Marguerite* (Theatre Royal Haymarket), *Marianne Dreams* (Almeida Theatre), *Bad Girls* (West Yorkshire Playhouse), *We Will Rock You* (Dominion Theatre), *Les Misérables* (Queens Theatre), Carmen (UK tour), *Castaway Case* (Edinburgh), *Whale Music* (Medena

Theatre). Television includes *The Song of Lunch*. Films include *Little Deaths, Well Prepared* and *The Man Who Met Himself* .

SAFFRON HOCKING | Te'o
Saffron trained at ALRA where she performed in *A Midsummer Night's Dream*, *Antony and Cleopatra* and *Arabian Nights* and was a Carleton Hobbs Bursary nominee for the radio plays *Sorrows and Rejoicings* by Athol Fugard and *Been So Long* by Che Walker.

ASH HUNTER | Ned Young
Theatre includes *Antony and Cleopatra* (RSC/ Public Theater New York), *Unrivalled Landscape* (Orange Tree Theatre), *God's Property* (Soho Theatre), *A Midsummer Night's Dream* (Almeida Theatre), *Gravity* (Birmingham Rep), *A Clockwork Orange* (Theatre Royal Stratford East). Television includes *Switch* and *Wolfblood*.

NAVEED KHAN | Menalee
Theatre includes *Pioneer* (Curious Directive/Watford Palace Theatre), *The Waiting Game* (Kazzum Arts), *59 Minutes to Save Christmas* (Slung Low with The

Barbican 2013 and The Cast 2014), *These Bones of Mine* and *After the Rainfall* (Curious Directive), *The Truth Teller* (King's Head), *The Tagore Project* (West Yorkshire Playhouse), *The Trial* (Watford Palace Theatre), *Lincoln Road* (Eastern Angles), *Jerusalem* (Oxford Playhouse). Films include *Second Coming* (2014) and *Survivor* (to be released in 2014). Trained at Oxford School of Drama.

CASSIE LAYTON | Mata
Cassie's theatre includes *Sense and Sensibility* (Watermill Theatre Newbury). Television includes *Saturdays*. Films include *Pylon* and *Jarhead 2*. Radio includes *Homefront*, *Chiwawa*, *The Divine Comedy*. She trained at RADA

ANNA LEONG BROPHY | Walua
Anna trained at East 15. Theatre includes *The Art of Fugue* (Soho Theatre), *The One Hour Plays (*The Matey Institute), *Shelf Life* (Theatre Delicatessen), *Paradise Street* (Futures Theatre), *Bewere* (Half Cut/ Latitude) and *Prometheus* (Secret Cinema). Films include *The Conversations*, *Are You Sophie?*, *A Kiss So Warm and Tender*, *GBH* and *Malaya: A Forgotten War*.

TOM MORLEY | Fletcher Christian
Theatre includes a gala reading of *The Seagull* for Out of Joint at the St James Theatre. Trained at LAMDA (graduated 2014) where he performed in *The School of Night, Sweeney Todd, The Revenger's Tragedy, The Lightening Play, Women Beware Women, Love and a Bottle, Elektra, Hamlet, The Wood Demon, For Services Rendered, The Way of the World* and *Iona Rain*.

ADAM NEWINGTON | John Adams
Adam has just graduated from the Royal Conservatoire of Scotland. Theatre includes *Dunsinane* (RSC/National Theatre of Scotland/UK Tour), *London 2012: Glasgow* (Traverse/Theatre Uncut), *Orpheus and Eurydice* (National Youth Theatre/Old Vic Tunnels), *The New World Order* (Hydrocracker/Barbican/Brighton Festival), *The Alchemist* (Minack Theatre).

HENRY PETTIGREW | William McKoy
Henry trained at Guildhall School of Music and Drama. Theatre includes *Of Mice and Men* (West Yorkshire Playhouse), *Straight* (Sheffield/Bush Theatre), *The Master and Margarita* (Complicité), *Anna Christie* (Donmar Warehouse), *Beautiful Burnout* (Frantic Assembly), *Hamlet* (Wyndham's Theatre), *Black Watch* (National Theatre of Scotland Tour of New York/LA/Barbican), *The Bevellers* (Citizens Theatre Glasgow), *Troilus and Cressida* (Edinburgh International Festival/RSC). Television includes *Shetland, Silent Witness, Line of Duty, Doctors, The Relief of Belsen* and *Midsomer Murders*.

DAVID RUBIN | Oha
Theatre includes, most recently, *Twelfth Night* (Liverpool Everyman re-opening). Also: *Hamlet, The Winter's Tale, Romeo and Juliet, Antony and Cleopatra, The Tempest, Julius Caesar* twice, *The Grain Store, American Trade, Morte D'Arthur, The Castle* (rehearsed reading), *A Mad World My Masters, Titus Andronicus,* (all RSC), *The Threepenny Opera, A Midsummer Night's Dream, The Red Balloon, As You Like It, Twelfth Night* and *The Tempest* (National Theatre), *The Lion, the Witch and the Wardrobe* (Kensington Palace), *Five Guys Named Moe* (West End), *Stomp* (Royal Festival Hall), *In The Midnight Hour Judd* (Young Vic), *Godspell* (Barbican), *Taylor's Dummies, The Overcoat* (Gecko), *Woyzech* (Omnibus), *Fight Face* and *Juicy Bits* (Lyric), *These Trees Are Made Of Blood* and *Sunday Morning* (BAC/Tara Arts), *Sleeping Beauty* (Stratford), *Company* and *Duck Variations* (Ipswich), *The Wizard of Oz* (Oldham Coliseum), *100* (Imaginary Body), *The Legend of King Arthur* (Red Shift), *Peter Pan* (Nuffield), *Cyrano de Bergerac* (Northampton), *Macbeth* (Chester), *Hamlet, Paula's Story, The Attraction* and many more as actor,

writer, director (Chickenshed). Television includes *The Passion, Walking With Cavemen, Sitting Pretty, Eastenders, Holby City, Dalziel and Pascoe, Mysteries of July, DJ Kat Show, Playdays, Zig-Zag, Watch, Number 73, Good Health.* Film includes *Brooms, Three Sheets to the Wind, Playing with Fire* and *Crossover.*

JACK TARLTON | William Brown
Jack trained at LAMDA and is an Artistic Associate of Presence Theatre for whom he conceived *The Animal (You).* Previously at Chichester: *Romeo and Juliet* (Festival Theatre). Other theatre includes *CHORALE – A Sam Shepard Roadshow: The Animal (You), The Holy Ghostly and The War in Heaven* (Presence Theatre & Actors Touring Company); *From Morning to Midnight, Coram Boy* and *Once in a Lifetime* (National Theatre); *A Doll's House, Rats' Tales* and *She Stoops to Conquer* (Royal Exchange Manchester), *Crave, Illusions* and *The Golden Dragon* (Actors Touring Company), *Beasts and Beauties* (Hampstead Theatre & Bristol Old Vic), *The Merchant of Venice, A Midsummer Night's Dream, Twelfth Night* and *The Taming of the Shrew* (Propeller), *The Deep Blue Sea* (Theatre Royal Bath Productions – Vaudeville Theatre), *The Sexual Neuroses of Our Parents* (The Gate), *The Man Who* (Orange Tree), *Gagarin Way* (Prime Cut), *Afore Night Come* (Young Vic), *An Inspector Calls* (Garrick Theatre), *Troilus and Cressida* and *A Month in the Country* (Royal Shakespeare Company). Television includes *Doctors, The Golden Hour, Dead Ringers, Doctor Who, The Genius of Mozart, Swivel on the Tip, Life Support, Wings of Angels* and *The Cater Street Hangman.* Films include *The Imitation Game, Nora* and *The Unscarred.*

THE CREATIVE TEAM

RICHARD BEAN | Writer
Richard Bean was born in Hull in 1956. After school, he worked in a bread plant before leaving to study Psychology at Loughborough University. Richard has worked as a psychologist and a stand-up comedian. Previously with Out of Joint: *The Big Fellah* (and Lyric Hammersmith). Other work for the stage includes: *Great Britain* (National Theatre); *One Man, Two Guvnors* (National Theatre/West End/Broadway/World Tour - winner, Evening Standard and Critics' Circle Awards for Best Play; Whatsonstage.com Award for Best New Comedy); a stage version of David Mamet's *The House of Games* (Almeida); *Pub Quiz is Life* (Hull Truck); *England People Very Nice* (National Theatre- Olivier Award Nomination for Best New Play); *The English Game* (Headlong); *Up On Roof* (Hull Truck - Nominated for TMA Play of the Year); *In The Club* (Hampstead Theatre); a version of Moliere's *The Hypochondriac* (Almeida); *The Heretic* (Royal Court - Evening Standard Award for Best Play); *Harvest* (Royal Court - Nominated for Evening Standard and Olivier Best New Play Awards, Winner Critics' Circle Best New Play); *Honeymoon Suite* (Royal Court - Pearson Play of the Year); *Under The Whaleback* (Royal Court - George Devine Award); *Toast* (Royal Court); *The God Botherers* (Bush Theatre); *Smack Family Robinson* (Live Theatre, Newcastle); *The Mentalists* (National Theatre); *Mr England* (Sheffield Crucible Theatre).

PANDA COX | Producer
Panda joined Out of Joint in 2009 as PA to Max Stafford-Clark, and became Deputy Producer in 2011. Independently she has produced *Tu I Teraz* (Here and Now) at Hampstead Theatre and Colchester Mercury Theatre earlier this year; and Jessica Swale's production of *The Palace of the End* for Red Handed at the Arcola in 2010. She was previously producer for Dancing Brick, and has worked with Escalator East to Edinburgh, Latitude Festival, and Norfolk & Norwich Festival.

GABRIELLE DAWES | Casting Director

Gabrielle is a freelance Casting Director, and an Associate of Chichester Festival Theatre. Other theatre at Chichester: over 30 productions including *Top Girls* (with Out of Joint), *King Lear* (and BAM New York), *The Resistible Rise of Arturo Ui, Singin' in the Rain, Private Lives, The Browning Version / South Downs, Yes, Prime Minister, Taking Sides / Collaboration* (all of which transferred to the West End), *Neville's Island, Top Girls* (and Trafalgar Studios), *Bingo* (and Young Vic) and *Macbeth* (and West End, BAM and Broadway). Also in Festival 2014 *Stevie, Pitcairn, Taken at Midnight, Frankie & Johnny in the Clair de Lune* and *An Ideal Husband*. Other theatre includes *Blithe Spirit, The King's Speech, Cat on a Hot Tin Roof, Three Days of Rain, A Round Heeled Woman, The Umbrellas of Cherbourg, Onassis, Treasure Island* (West End), *The Norman Conquests* (Old Vic and Broadway), *All About My Mother* (Old Vic), productions for Hampstead Theatre, Headlong, Theatre Royal Bath and Sheffield, *Caroline, or Change, Elmina's Kitchen, The Pillowman* and *Coram Boy* (National Theatre 2000-2006). Television credits include *Macbeth* directed by Rupert Goold, Harold Pinter's *Celebration, Elmina's Kitchen* by Kwame Kwei-Armah. Films include *Perdie* (BAFTA award for Best Short Film) and *The Suicide Club*.

ANDRZEJ GOULDING | Video Designer

Also for Chichester in 2014: *Pressure* (Minerva Theatre and Lyceum Edinburgh). Theatre credits include Video and set design for *Union* (Royal Lyceum Theatre Edinburgh), *The Last Witch* (Edinburgh International Festival) and *Sane New World* (Ruby Wax UK Tour). Video design includes *Peter Grimes* (Grange Park Opera), *Relative Values* (West End/Theatre Royal Bath), *Hannah* (Unicorn), *Fanciulla Del West, Joshua* (Opera North), *Coriolanus* (Donmar Warehouse), *From Morning to Midnight* (National Theatre), *Groove On Down the Road* (Zoo Nation), *The Machine* (Manchester International Festival), *Relative Values* (Theatre Royal Bath), *Othello* (Singapore Rep), *Carousel* (Théâtre du Châtelet/Opera North), *Silent Night* (Philadelphia Opera/Minnesota Opera), *Our House Concert* (Savoy Theatre), *Amadeus* (Maltz Jupiter Theatre Florida), *Peter Pan* (Sherman Cardiff), *Mass Observation* (Almeida Festival), *DNA* (Hull Truck), *Maria* (Wexford Opera House), *Orlando* (Glasgow Opera House/Festival Theatre Edinburgh), *Enlightenment* (Hampstead), *Speed the Plow* (The Old Vic), *Varjak Paw* (Linbury Studio UK Tour). Video animation work includes *Ghost the Musical* (Manchester Opera House, Piccadilly Theatre, UK Tour), *Love Never Dies* (Adelphi Theatre), *Alice's Adventures in Wonderland* (Royal Opera House). Trained in Theatre Design at Central Saint Martins, London.

TIM HOARE | Associate Director

Tim is currently Associate Director for Out of Joint. Previously at Chichester: Director for *Fred's Diner* (world premiere. Theatre on the Fly); Associate Director on *Yes, Prime Minster* (and West End and National Tour) and *Alice in Wonderland* (both Festival Theatre); Assistant Director for *Pygmalion* (Festival Theatre), *South Downs/The Browning Version* (and West End), *Top Girls* (also with Out of Joint; and West End) and *The Master Builder* (all Minerva Theatre), Trainee Director at Chichester Festival Theatre (2010-12) and Artistic Director for Theatre on the Fly. Theatre credits include as Director *Such, Such Were the Joys* (NT Studio), *Masterpieces* (Royal Court Theatre Upstairs: Surprise Theatre Season), *What People Do* (Old Vic Tunnels), *Number 1* (Bush Theatre), *Henry V* (Trafalgar Studios and National Theatre Tbilisi Georgia) and *Bash* (Barons Court Theatre); as Associate Director *This May Hurt a Bit* (Out of Joint/Octagon Theatre Bolton tour and St James Theatre) and *Our Country's Good* (Out of Joint/Octagon Theatre Bolton international tour); as Assistant Director *King Lear* (National Theatre), *Eigenrau* (Bush Theatre) and *Slaves* (Theatre 503). Studied at Balliol College Oxford and British American Drama Academy.

EMMA LAXTON | Sound Designer

Future productions include *Cat On a Hot Tin Roof* (Royal Exchange, Royal & Derngate and Northern

Stage). Recent Theatre credits include *Saints* (Nuffield), *The Colby Sisters of Pittsburgh* (Tricycle Theatre), *Pests, The Westbridge The Heretic, Tusk Tusk, Faces in the Crowd, Gone Too Far!, Incomplete, Random Acts of Kindness, My Name is Rachel Corrie, Food Chain* (Royal Court Theatre), *The Blackest Black* and *#AIWW: The Arrest of Ai Wei Wei, Lay Down Your Cross* and *Blue Heart Afternoon* (Hampstead Theatre), *Coriolanus, Berenice, The Physicists, Making Noise Quietly, The Recruiting Officer* (Donmar Warehouse), *All My Sons, A Doll's House, Three Birds, The Accrington Pals, Lady Windermere's Fan* (Royal Exchange), *Much Ado About Nothing* (The Old Vic), *nut, Men Should Weep* (National Theatre), *Henry the Fifth* (Unicorn), *OMG!* (Sadler's Wells/The Place), *The Promise* (Donmar Warehouse at Trafalgar Studios), *The Sacred Flame* (English Touring Theatre), *Black T-Shirt Collection* (Fuel UK Tour and National Theatre), *Invisible* (Transport UK Tour and Luxembourg), *Much Ado About Nothing* (Wyndhams Theatre West End), *Pornography* (Birmingham Rep, Traverse and Tricycle Theatre). Emma is the Associate Sound Designer of *War Horse* and was an Associate Artist at the Bush Theatre.

ORIAN MICHAELI | Choreographer
Theatre credits include as Choreographer: *This May Hurt a Bit* (Out of Joint) and *Mouth Piece* (Amy Nostbakken). Choreographer/Dancer: *To the Past* (Israeli Reality Festival Jerusalem, Acco Theatre and Tmuna Theatre Tel-Aviv) and *Talented Like a Demon* (Jewish Summer Festival Budapest/Red Shell Festival Tel-Aviv/ Acco Theatre). Dancer/Deviser: *Lady Dog* (Tmuna Theatre/Suzan Dala Theatre Tel-Aviv), *Glory Monster* (Kipla Theatre and Beit Tami Tel-Aviv, Tiberius Cultural Centre, Eilat Cultural Centre and Yavne Theatre), *DayDreams* (Acco Festival, Nahmani Theatre and Suzan Dalal Theatre Tel-Aviv and Acco Theatre), *Biaur* (Acco Festival and Suzan Dalal Theatre Tel-Aviv). Actress/Dancer/Acrobat: *The Observatory* (Israel Festival/Tbilisi International Theatre Festival). Actress: *Treasures in the Wall*, Actress/Choreographer: *The Tired Hero* (Acco Theatre). Actress/Deviser: *Waiting for Zoro* (Klipa Theatre Tel-Aviv). Choreographer/Deviser: *Ballad of the Burning Star* (Theatre Ad Infinitum). Films include *Goose Pumps, It's Not All That Simple* and *Fairy on the Roof*. Winner of the Keren Sharet Foundation Scholarship and the Lohamei Hagetaot Museum Award.

ADAM PLEETH | Composer
Adam composed music for *This May Hurt A Bit* (Out of Joint and Octagon Theatre Bolton), *Entries on Love* and *Time Stands Still When I Think of You*. As composer and performer: *The Elephantom* (National Theatre), *Ballad of the Burning Star* (Theatre Ad Infinitum), *Juana in a Million* and *The Adventures of Curious Ganz* (Silent Tide). As a musician: *Brief counter* (Kneehigh), *Cinderella* (Travelling Light) and *Babel* (Wildworks).

RICHARD RYDER | Dialect Coach
Richard Ryder has worked in the voice departments of the RSC and the National Theatre. He has just released an accent app for actors called 'The Accent Kit', a free download at the app store. His work in theatre includes *A Streetcar Names Desire* (Young Vic), *A Taste of Honey, Blurred Lines, Protest Song, 50 Years on Stage, Emil and the Detectives, Home, Romeo and Juliet, Untold Stories, Table, This House, Port, The Captain of Köpenick, Cocktail Sticks* and *Hymn* (National Theatre), *The Tempest* and *The Merchant of Venice* (RSC), *American Psycho* and *The Turn of the Screw* (Almeida), *Fatal Attraction* (Theatre Royal Haymarket), *Fings Ain't What They Used To Be* and *Oh! What a Lovely War* (Theatre Royal Stratford East), *Billy Liar* and *Wonderful Town* (Manchester Royal Exchange), *The Duck House* and *Uncle Vanya* (Vaudeville Theatre), *Barking in Essex* (Wyndham's Theatre), *Race and Hysteria* (Hampstead Theatre), *Paper Doll, Red Velvet* and *The Colby Sisters of Pittsburgh* (Tricycle), *Road to Mecca, In Skagway, Moby Dick* and *But I cd only whisper* (Arcola), *Proof* (Menier Chocolate Factory), *The Winslow Boy* (The Old Vic), *One Monkey Don't Stop No Show* (Eclipse Theatre), *The Thirty-Nine Steps* (Criterion

Theatre and Tour), *The History Boys*, *My Fair Lady* and *A Taste of Honey* (Sheffield Crucible), *The Kingdom* (Soho Theatre), *Beautiful Burnout* (Frantic Assembly), *A View From the Bridge* and *The Norman Conquests* (Liverpool Everyman), *Twist of Gold* (Polka Theatre), *It Just Stopped* (Orange Tree). www.therichervoice.com www.theaccentkit.com

TIM SHORTALL | Designer

Previously for Out of Joint and Chichester: *Top Girls*. Previously for Out of Joint: *This May Hurt A Bit* and *Our Country's Good* (Out of Joint/Octagon Theatre Bolton, Tour and St James Theatre), The Big Fellah (with Lyric Hammersmith), King of Hearts (with Hampstead Theatre); The Overwhelming (National Theatre in association with Out of Joint; also Roundabout Theater New York). Also for Chichester: Dead Funny. Also for Shakespeare's Globe: A New World. Other theatre includes set for *La Cage aux Folles* (West End, US Tour, and on Broadway. Tony nomination for Best Design of a Musical), Awake and Sing (Almeida), *The Philanthropist* (Donmar and Broadway), *900 Oneonta* (The Old Vic), *Disappeared* (Royal Court), set for *Sweet Charity* (Theatre Royal Haymarket, Menier Chocolate Factory), *Race, Old Money* (Hampstead), *These Shining Lives* (Park Theatre), *Educating Rita* and *Rookery Nook* (Menier Chocolate Factory), *Amen Corner* (Tricycle), *Excuses* (Soho Theatre), *Haunted* (Arts Theatre), *The Colonel Bird* (Gate Theatre), Robots (Barclays TMA award nomination, Best Design). West End: *Whipping It Up* and *Telstar* (Ambassadors), *See How They Run* (Duchess), *Elton John's Glasses* (Queens), *Body and Soul* and costumes for *The Big Knife* (Albery), *Murder by Misadventure* (Vaudeville). Dance *Private City/Track and Field* (Sadler's Wells Royal Ballet), *Sonata in Time* (Scottish Ballet), *Rhyme Nor Reason* and *Party Game* (Norwegian National Ballet), *The Nightingale* (Dutch National Ballet). Television *20th Century Blues*, *The Nightingale* (Prix Italia RAI Prize for Best Design).

JAKE SMITH | Assistant Director

Jake Smith is a Trainee Director at Chichester Festival Theatre and this season was Assistant Director on *Miss Julie/Black Comedy* (Minerva Theatre). He began his career at Hull Truck Theatre and was a founding member of Assemble Fest an ACE funded Street Theatre Festival in Hull promoting, mentoring and supporting emerging theatre companies. Theatre credits as Director include *The Little Match Girl* (site specific), *Alice's Site* (Hull Truck) and *The Coronation of Poppea* (Middleton Hall); as Assistant Director *Whale Music* (Hull Truck) and *The Last Days of Youth* (Teatru Radu Stanca). He studied Drama and Theatre Practice at the University of Hull graduating with First-class honours.

MAX STAFFORD-CLARK | Director

Educated at Trinity College, Dublin, Max Stafford-Clark co-founded Joint Stock Theatre Group in 1974 following his Artistic Directorship of The Traverse Theatre, Edinburgh. From 1979 to 1993 he was Artistic Director of The Royal Court Theatre. In 1993 he founded Out of Joint. His work as a director has overwhelmingly been with new writing, and he has commissioned and directed first productions from writers including Sue Townsend, Stephen Jeffreys, Timberlake Wertenbaker, Sebastian Barry, April de Angelis, Mark Ravenhill, Andrea Dunbar, Robin Soans, Alistair Beaton, Stella Feehily, Sebastian Barry, David Hare and Caryl Churchill. Revivals include *The Seagull*, *The Recruiting Officer* and *King Lear* (Royal Court), *A Jovial Crew*, *The Wives' Excuse* and *The Country Wife* (RSC), and *The Man of Mode*, *She Stoops to Conquer*, *Three Sisters* and *Macbeth* (Out of Joint). He directed David Hare's *The Breath of Life* for Sydney Theatre Company, *The Overwhelming* for New York's Roundabout Theatre and most recently *The Seagull* for Culture Project (also NY). Max holds honorary doctorates from Oxford Brookes, Warwick and Hertfordshire universities, and Visiting Professorships at Hertfordshire, Warwick and York. His books are *Letters to George*, *Taking Stock*, *Our Country's Good Page to Stage* and *Journal of the Plague Year*.

JOHANNA TOWN | Lighting Designer

Johanna has lit over 20 productions with Out of Joint including *Our Country's Good, The Steward of Christendom, Macbeth* and *The Permanent Way*. Previously at Chichester: *The Deep Blue Sea* and *Nijinsky* (Festival Theatre) and *In Praise of Love* (Minerva Theatre). Other credits include *Fences, What the Butler Saw, Some Like It Hip Hop, Betrayal, Speaking in Tongues, Beautiful Thing* (West End), *Tonight @ 8.30* (Nuffield/ETT), *Love Your Soldiers, The Pride, That Face* (Sheffield), *To Sir With Love* (Northampton), *All My Sons* (Manchester/Talawa), *Smack Family Robinson* (Kingston), *Joking Apart* (Salisbury/Nottingham), *Medea, Romeo and Juliet* (Headlong/UK Tour), *Blue Sky, Blue Heart Afternoon* (Hampstead), *Straight* (Bush/Sheffield), *The Norman Conquests* (Liverpool), *Moon on a Rainbow Shawl* (NT/Talawa/UK Tour), *Miss Julie, A View From the Bridge, Beautiful Thing* (Manchester), *Haunted* (Royal Exchange/ NY/Sydney), *Llywyth* (Sherman Cymru), *Charged* (Soho), *The Tragedy of Thomas Hobbes* (RSC), *Rose* (NT/Broadway), *My Name is Rachel Corrie* (Royal Court/West End/NY), *Arabian Nights, Our Lady of Sligo* (NY), *Guantanamo* (NY/Tricycle/West End). Johanna is an Associate Artist for Theatre 503 where credits include *The Life of Stuff* (Offie nomination, Best Lighting Designer). Opera includes *Porgy and Bess* (Royal Danish Opera), *Ottello* (Nice Opera House), *Carmen, Kátya Kabanová, Secret Marriage* (Scottish Opera), *The Marriage of Figaro* (Classical Opera Company).

JONATHAN WALLER | Fight Director

Previously at Chichester *The Recruiting Officer* (Festival Theatre). Extensive theatre credits include *The Play That Goes Wrong* (Mischief Theatre/Kenny Wax), *Richard II* and *Twelfth Night* (Shakespeare's Globe on Broadway), *Between Empires* (Orange Tree/ Edinburgh Festival), *'Tis Pity She's a Whore* and *Macbeth* (Cheek by Jowl), *Four Nights in Knaresborough* and *The Canterbury Tales* (Southwark Playhouse), *Love's Labour's Lost, Romeo and Juliet, Richard III*, Edward II and *Richard II* (Shakespeare's Globe), *Mad Forest* and *Romeo and Juliet* (BAC), *Where There's a Will, Far From the Madding Crowd, The Changeling* and *Mother Courage* (ETT), *They Have Oak Trees in North Carolina* (Tristan Bates Theatre), *Rough Crossings* (Headlong), *Alpha Beta* (NT Studio), *Some Voices* (Young Vic). Television/documentaries include *Pride and Prejudice, Five Children and It, Soldiers, Renaissance, Timewatch – William Marshall, The Birth of Europe, Nature by Design, Warrior School, Tipping the Velvet, Blood and Bullets, Reclaiming the Blade, Bronze Age War, Hinterland* and *Wolf Hall*. Films include *Robin Hood, First Knight* and *Ladder of Swords*. Jonathan is founder member and teacher of The European Historical Combat Guild and a teaching member of the British Academy of Dramatic Combat. He teaches at LAMDA, Guildhall School of Music and Drama, Rutgers University BA Acting London Program/Shakespeare's Globe and Boston University BA Acting London Program.

Characters

Mutineers

Fletcher Christian

Ned Young

Matthew Quintal

William McKoy

William Brown

John Adams

Polynesian Women (their 'husbands' in brackets)

Walua (Matthew Quintal)

Te'o (William McKoy)

Mata (Ned Young)

Mi Mitti (Fletcher Christian)

Te Lahu (William Brown)

Fasto (Oha/John Adams)

Polynesian Men

Menalee

Hiti

Oha

Marines and Officers

Captain Pipon

Captain Staines

Calvert (Marine)

Magee (Marine)

Pratt (Marine)

Set

Pitcairn Island. A fist of volcanic rock thrusting out from an expanse of Pacific. It is not a welcoming island. The Pacific crashes against sheer cliffs which rise hundreds of feet from the sea. No sense of a beach, nothing is gentle.

The playing area is the fertile plateau above Bounty Bay. Up stage is a cliff top beyond which is a sea and sky horizon.

Stage right, and high, is a cave, an eyrie. A path to the eyrie snakes down to the playing area.

This text went to press before the end of rehearsals and so may differ slightly from the play as performed.

PROLOGUE 1

1814. A clearing surrounded by trees. Enter a group of English marines with muskets cocked, ready, casually nervous. There is a basket of collected coconuts. CAPTAIN PIPON and CAPTAIN STAINES follow.

PRATT: This island's got life sir. Look, someone's gathered these here coconuts.

PIPON: And someone made the basket.

PRATT: Oh aye. That kind o' thinking'll be how you made officer.

MAGEE: I'll wager I'll find a rum tree in a minute.

CALVERT: It's a damned paradise!

PRATT: Shh!

Silence.

Wood smoke sir.

STAINES: You can hear wood smoke?

PRATT: Smell it sir.

CALVERT: We're on the village.

STAINES: Company! Consider! Fletcher Christian, has nothing to lose, he knows he will hang. They were young men when they took the Bounty, so they're old now, yes, but not too old to fight. Not all the men were active mutineers so no firing, except in self–defence.

MATA appears, she has a musket raised. MATA wears a large wooden cross around her neck. She is seen by the Marines but not the officers.

Our aim is to secure the men, alive, and return them to court martial –

CALVERT: – Sir?!

STAINES: I doubt they still have powder but if they have had peace in this garden of Eden then their reserves may yet be plenty.

1

MATA: Yoo kah pahs!

STAINES: Lord Almighty?!

MAGEE raises his musket.

PIPON: No firing!

MATA: Wosing yourley doon?

PIPON: *(To STAINES.)* It's not English.

CALVERT: It is sir. 'What are you doing?'

PIPON: We wish to speak with Fletcher Christian.

The other women now appear. They are all either pregnant or carrying babies at the breast. All have wooden crosses around their necks.

MAGEE: Strewth!

STAINES: Greetings! English! Friendly!

PIPON: Magee! Stop pointing that musket!

STAINES: Where are your husbands?

TE LAHU: Es wuhn man.

CALVERT: Is one man.

STAINES: What is this man's name?

TE LAHU: Adam.

PIPON: Fletcher Christian, is he dead?

MI MITTI: Titreano?

CALVERT: *(To PIPON.)* Titreano is the name they gave Christian on Tahiti sir.

MI MITTI: Ai ka wes Titreano –

MATA and FASTO pull MI MITTI to the back of the group.

TE LAHU: – *(Louder.)* Titreano dead uz hatchet long time.

CALVERT: *(Pedantically.)* Christian has been dead as a hatchet for a long time, sir.

PIPON: I've got the measure of it now thank you Calvert.

Enter a middle-aged man, though looking much older with wild hair and a sun hat obscuring his face. He is carried by four women in a kind of sedan chair arrangement. He has a Bible on his lap. They put the sedan chair down.

MUTINEER: *(Cockney.)* You come all this way to hang me then have yer lads!

STAINES: Not summarily.

PIPON: Captain Philip Pipon. HMS Tagus.

STAINES: Captain Thomas Staines. HMS Briton.

MUTINEER: John Adams.

PIPON: Your rank?

MUTINEER: AB.

STAINES: Your ship?

MUTINEER: H.M.A.V. Bounty. Welcome to Pitcairn's Island. Fasto! Wickles for everyone. Jump to it girl! And summat to slake the thirst of these officers!

PIPON: Calvert! Take the company through to the village.

MUTINEER: They'll spoil you. Aye.

PIPON: How much might they spoil them?

MUTINEER: You got an imagination son. Na! They're all God fearing. I learned 'em all in the way of the book ain't I.

The marines follow the women off. MUTINEER, PIPON and STAINES are left alone.

STAINES: You are the one remaining man on the island?

MUTINEER: Aye. What of Bligh? Does he live?

PIPON: He does.

MUTINEER: I said he'd make land! God Bless Him! That morning on the Bounty, I were in me cot, and I come up when all Bedlam broke out. Bligh sees me and sends me back down to get his

3

breeches, to cover his modesty, which, being
loyal and innocent of all schemes, I did. Is he
here? Bligh?

STAINES: No. He has another commission.

MUTINEER: Joseph Banks and the breadfruit?

STAINES: Yes.

MUTINEER: Kaw! Bligh loves that damned bread fruit don't he?!

STAINES: What happened to the Master's Mate, Christian?

MUTINEER: Has there ever, in the history of all England,
been a more unfortunate man? Eh? A gentleman
of Westmorland, an officer, he coulda been an
ornament to his country but in them first six
months on Tahiti the Lord tempted him his fruit
and like Adam in the Garden he didn't have
no chance, and he left the righteous path of the
Lord and turned to Venus.

STAINES: Lust?

MUTINEER: I think he thought it were love, the two are easily
confused. Not being quarter deck meself I never
got near enough to be sure.

STAINES: But he's dead? Fletcher Christian?

MUTINEER: Over twenty year back. Aye, a terrible gripe, laid
all the lads low.

PIPON: All but you.

MUTINEER: I'm blessed with me father's blood, the only
thing he ever give me worth having. He was a
waterman on the Thames, and picked up every
disease the devil's invented, and never had a day
in bed. Aye, a gripe laid all the lads low,
until one day the sun comes up and I was the
only man standing. That were twenty year back.
By my reckoning I'm forty-nine. I know, I look
older, that's the women.

End of scene.

ACT 1
SCENE 1

A clearing on the plateau. The sound of dogs barking. MATTHEW QUINTAL leads the men in singing Shantyman style, improvising lines as he goes. On each Haul Away! they take a step back, which brings them slowly on to the stage. Hauling the rope are WILLIAM MCKOY, JOHN ADAMS, MATTHEW QUINTAL and the Polynesians MENALEE, OHA and the boy HITI. HITI wears a union jack flag as a kind of toga. The Brits are tattooed with Polynesian style tattoos and all look to have gone a bit native with shell necklaces and the like. QUINTAL is the most extreme – he wears only a loin cloth. FLETCHER CHRISTIAN is high in the eyrie, he's writing, working on what looks like a document, or a speech. The team are hauling a sled laden with valuable goods recovered from the Bounty. The women run on and off to the bathing pool, but return to the fire as a base as the food is being prepared there. There is the consistent background noise of dogs barking from below.

QUINTAL: *In South West England I was born*

ALL: Heave away! Haul away!

QUINTAL: *To Tahiti round Cape Horn*

ALL: We're bound for O Tahiti
Haul away you rolling King
Heave away! Haul away!
All the way you'll hear me sing
We're bound for O Tahiti

QUINTAL: *On that isle met a native lass*

Some laughter, some yeahs!

ALL: Heave away! Haul away!

QUINTAL: *her body's shaped like an hour glass*

More laughter.

ALL: We're bound to O Tahiti

QUINTAL: *I shook her up I shook her down (More laughter.)*

ALL: Heave away! Haul away!

QUINTAL: *There's none like her in Deptford town*

5

ALL: We're bound to O'Tahiti
       Haul away you rolling King
       Heave away! Haul away!
       All the way you'll hear me sing
       We're bound to O'Tahiti

Enter WALUA, TE'O, TE LAHU, and MATA. QUINTAL drops the rope and goes over to WALUA for a grope and a kiss.

NED: *(Off.)* McKoy! What's the damned problem?!

MCKOY: Our shanty man's got a prick for brains!

QUINTAL: Get us some water you little coney! Go on!
       Damn it, I'm beat, bone tired.

The girls run off, QUINTAL sits and leches after them, gets a wave from WALUA.

MCKOY: Yous won't need rocking to sleep tonight then.

QUINTAL: I'll find some blood for that one.

Enter NED YOUNG. He is wearing an officer's jacket.

NED: You can sit when the work's done Quintal.

QUINTAL: I'll sweat as much as any land-owning squire in
       England, and no damned long pelt of a
       blackamoor bitch is gonna lash me on me own
       island.

They square off. The rope starts to slip.

ADAMS: Oi! She's slipping down.

QUINTAL stands his ground so NED takes up some of the rope.

NED: McKoy, call us a shanty.

QUINTAL: *(Singing.) That bastard Bligh he lashed me twice!*

ALL: Heave away! Haul away!

QUINTAL: *they'll lash me no more in my life*
       I'm bound to Pitcairn's Island

ALL: Haul away you rolling King

Heave away! Haul away!
All the way you'll hear me sing
We're bound to Pitcairn's Island

The work is done. The sled secured. The girls come back with water. The men sit and drink. MATA gives HITI a half coconut. He is smitten. He drinks the milk walking forwards for direct address, and fourth wall breaking engagement with the audience.

HITI: I was surfing on my island, Tubuai, my island
        called Tubai, not Tahiti. I am from Tubai, not
        Tahiti. Understand? Do you understand?
        Where am I from? *(Tubai.)* Which is not?
        (Tahiti.) You are intelligent and will be wealthy.
        When you grow up. With many pigs. Surfing is
        my favourite thing. We Polynesians invented
        surfing, and swimming. I saw three trees where
        the sky meets the sea. I know it is the three masts
        of an English ship because when I was a small
        small boy King Toote came to my island *(Tubai.)*
        Who is King Toote? *(Captain Cook.)* Yes, very
        clever. You will be wealthy when you grow up
        with many pigs. And King Toote touched my
        head with his hand, and did like that with my
        hair. Like that. So when I saw the trees I ran
        down to the beach. My island..?..*(Tubuai.)* has a
        beach, white, beautiful, not like here. Only one
        good thing about Pitcairn, no flies.

MATA walks by teasing him. He places his hand on his penis. Just placed, no frottage.

        Two good things about Pitcairn. No flies and
        Mataohu. She makes me hard. She's seventeen.
        I'm fifteen. Mmmm. The ship was called His
        Majesty's Armed Vessel Bounty, but no flag.
        It was not King Toote it was Titreano. In English
        Fletcher Christian, but we say Titreano. Can
        you say Titreano? *(Titreano.)* Beautiful. You will
        be wealthy when you grow up with many pigs.
        Titreano had a coat with iron buttons. We don't

7

have iron on my island, it is wonderful, iron,
I love it.

He points up to FLETCHER CHRISTIAN.

Titreano made me his taio, which is blood friend
until death. He gave me porter to drink, which
tastes like piss, and makes you sick, very good.
He then give me an iron button, look, beautiful,
but no jacket, not yet. Maybe soon. Titreano
gave me a job on The Bounty as an AB which
means 'nearly a God'. I asked my mother if
I could go sail away with Titreano and her
advice was 'always kill the fish before you eat
it'. What do you think that means? I had no
idea, so here I am now on Matakitereangi,
but because I am now English, I will call it
Pitcairn. Not Pitcairn Island, you don't say
England Island do you, no, just Pitcairn.

QUINTAL: Where's my dog Alex Smith? A country squire
needs a damned dog for his dirty acres.

ADAMS: All them dogs is locked in the chart room. Ain't
nofin to do wi' me.

QUINTAL looks up at CHRISTIAN who is scanning the horizon.

QUINTAL: If Bligh turns up here with a Man O'War, we
could defend this island.

MCKOY: That stinking Jesuit's dead and rotting in hell.

NED: Wouldn't surprise me if he's back in Deptford
right now, fitting out a prison ship with manacles
for seven.

ADAMS: Six.

QUINTAL: 'cause you was sick in your hammock, want yer?
Slept right through the whole watch didn't yer?
Woke up in the morning to a new captain.

ADAMS: Aye, that's it.

MCKOY: You're as tarred as any of us Alex Smith,
and Bligh he seen you too, aye.

QUINTAL: I heard him whisper your name as he climbed
into the launch. 'Alex Smith', 'Alex Smith'.
He was stowing your name away ready for the
Admirals.

ADAMS: I'll be alright then 'cause Alex Smith ain't my name.

QUINTAL: Reckless Jack that's your name!

MCKOY: If you're nae Alex Smith who are ye? Bonny
Prince Charlie?

*Enter William BROWN. BROWN is carrying a notebook. He is dressed
not as a seaman, but as a gardener.*

BROWN: Mister Young, sir! Wonderful news!

QUINTAL: You've found some more women?

BROWN: I thought it unsupposable, but this land has been
populated before! The land was farmed, and is
planted with many different species –

OHA and MENALEE address the women, ignoring the mutineers.

OHA: *(To the other Polynesians.)* Their gardener is saying
what I was saying on the ship, our people have
lived on this island here before.

MENALEE: This is the lost island of Matakiterangi?

The Polynesians gather round. Excluding the English.

MCKOY: Oi! Mammu Mammu!

QUINTAL: Speak English!

NED: Menalee, what is all this excitement?

MENALEE: Owuz folk back afore.

OHA: Plenty marae, yus ken?

MENALEE: Marae. Stone, stone, stone, stone.

NED: A temple?

MENALEE:/OHA: Eyeuh!!

BROWN: There's breadfruit, coconuts, yams, plantains, two different types of banana and the Mulberry tree for cloth. We can make clothes!

QUINTAL: I got no plans to wear no damned clothes.

BROWN: Where is Mister Christian?

NED: On his watch.

NED indicates where CHRISTIAN is and BROWN heads off to tell him the news. Enter MI MITTI, tall and superior, she's just bathed.

QUINTAL: Eh up lads! The Queen's coming. Stand to attention. Mine already is! Strewth, look at that, she gets me all venereal. I'm gonna tup her, if it takes my last breath.

NED: Quintal, I'll counsel you to leave Christian's girl alone.

QUINTAL: Go wipe. And I'll counsel you Ned Young not to build your house too near me. I don't want to keep you awake at nights.

NED: And what is it that might disturb me?

QUINTAL: The sound of my balls slapping again' her arse.

NED walks down and joins MI MITTI. He sits.

NED: Mi Mitti, I see you found a bathing pool.

MI MITTI: Eeyeuh! No flies.

NED: You must be on your guard against Mister Quintal.

MI MITTI: I am ra'atira. He knows he cannot speak to me.

NED: He considers all the rules are now rewrit, and I'm afraid the fact of you being high born will not constrain his behaviour.

CHRISTIAN approaches.

NED: *(To CHRISTIAN.)* This is the last sled. The ship is voided.

CHRISTIAN: What of the boats?

NED: The jolly boat and the canoe are hauled and secured above the tide.

CHRISTIAN: Have the people had their ration?

NED: Not yet.

CHRISTIAN: Hold it back.

NED: I can't control them, and now that the work is done they will want to take their pleasures with the women.

CHRISTIAN: No! The 'House' must sit tonight, and sober.

NED: The Lords or Commons sir?

CHRISTIAN: The Lords and Commons as one. I plan to open the meeting by taking off my uniform. I will place it on the fire, and then ask you to take off your tunic and do like wise.

NED: I know of no successful society that does not have some vestige of hierarchy.

CHRISTIAN: This levelling is more painful for us. The men are trading the short, brutal, scurvy ridden, life of an AB for a cottage in Arcadia.

NED: With respect sir, you and I are not equal in sacrifice. Your family were already bankrupted and their lands on the Isle of Man taken in lieu before you could have your portrait painted. This contrasts with my fortune on St Kitts which is intact.

CHRISTIAN: Brutal.

NED: Now is the time for truths. Before your Parliament of the people further depletes, by enclosure, what little of the earth is left to me.

CHRISTIAN: I count it a blessing, that my family were bankrupted before my portrait was painted. My mother might forget me more easily.

NED: Mine must suffer, I have two portraits.

CHRISTIAN: Don't speak of this with my wife. She naturally presumes that as an officer I'm heir to a fortune.

NED: She will find your ideas of equality difficult.

CHRISTIAN: Perhaps, but the division between quarter deck and forecastle cannot continue.

NED: Why not?

CHRISTIAN: Because this island is a new leaf. Why foul it with tradition?

NED: Easy to say when you've lost your fortune.

CHRISTIAN: Your fortune may be extant on St. Kitts, but you will never see it again. You will see a rope sooner.

NED: So what are the principles of this levelling?

CHRISTIAN: Reason and individualism. Our age has gifted us with thinkers that have shown us a rational approach to life and nature, allowing us to question faith and tradition. Spinoza –

NED: – A Jew?

CHRISTIAN: He was excommunicated from the synagogue –

NED: – so a nobody and a Jew.

CHRISTIAN: God did not give us Pitcairn? I found it by reason, by charts, by science!

NED: I prayed every night.

CHRISTIAN: You know the truth. There was no celestial hand.

NED: What of God, here?

CHRISTIAN: Imagine life without the clergy!? When we were in Tenerife I discussed with a French officer,

a prisoner on The Daffodil, and he told me
that there is a movement to raise the third estate,
the serfs, and this thinking comes from the
aristocracy! He said that in his lifetime he
expected all men in his country to be equal.

NED: They'd still be French. We are both gentlemen,
I expect no less from the division of this island
than you.

CHRISTIAN: And I will have no more than any man.

NED: Then I will take my reduction in good heart.

CHRISTIAN: Such gloom! We have everything we need!

NED: We have no physician.

CHRISTIAN: Are you ill?

NED: Not yet.

CHRISTIAN: We shall live better here than on rations.
Ned, one last order, before we abdicate all
authority, we must have the dogs killed.
Their barking will betray us.

NED: They can't be heard in Deptford.

CHRISTIAN: If a ship arrives, they'll give us away.

NED: Quintal won't take kindly to the killing of his
dog.

CHRISTIAN: What is his mood?

NED: Foul. As ever.

CHRISTIAN: I blame myself, for Quintal.

NED: Are you mother or father?

CHRISTIAN: When the pressed men ran, Bligh sent me out
to recruit, under oath not to disclose our
destination. I found McKoy and Quintal in a
tavern. I couldn't sway them, initially, and then
I said the word.

NED: Tahiti.

CHRISTIAN: Since Cook Tahitian girls have ousted mermaids in every sailor's imagination.

A scream as QUINTAL starts urinating in front of the girls.

NED: And yet from today, Quintal is my equal?

CHRISTIAN: And not just Quintal.

NED: There is someone lower?

CHRISTIAN: The natives.

NED: *(Laughs.)* This is sceptical!

CHRISTIAN: You, yourself, as a quadroon, are one quarter native.

NED: And three quarters English gentleman. Do you have plans to enfranchise the women?

CHRISTIAN: Ned, I'm not mad.

NED: I no longer know what to expect. What was revolutionary yesterday, today is Tory policy.

CHRISTIAN: Muster the crew and the chiefs at dusk on the log there, in this clearing. This will be our Parliament.

NED: There will be violence if the men perceive their station undercut. Put your equality proposals before the crew alone, and let them decide.

CHRISTIAN: *(He considers.)* Very well. But kill the dogs first.

CHRISTIAN turns and goes to the fire and gets himself some food and water. The men disperse. The women are gathered around the fire. A pot is cooking. MI MITTI, TE LAHU, WALUA, TE'O, FASTO and MATA.

NED: Rum and pleasures will be delayed this evening!

QUINTAL: Go wipe your arse! Walua! Girl! I'm gonna dock you all the darkmans!

WALUA giggles.

NED: No drinking! There are decisions to be made. At the log. Sober. On the bell! Hiti!

QUINTAL exits. HITI comes over.

HITI: Aye sir!

Ned   Because of your brave and constant service
           Titreano has promoted you to 'Midshipman',
           which means 'at God's right hand'. This tunic
           is yours.

NED takes off his naval tunic and gives it to HITI, who puts it on, it's way too big.

HITI: Tank yoo sir!

NED: The dogs are locked in the Bounty's chart room.
           Go back down to her, and –

HITI: – her? Who her?

NED: A ship in the English navy is a she, a her,
           because like a woman if you look after her,
           she'll look after you. It'll make sense when
           you're older.

HITI: Aye, aye, sir.

He hands over a key.

NED: Kill the dogs.

HITI: Ah like em dogs.

NED: Hiti, when a sailor says 'aye, aye sir' what does
           it mean?

HITI: First cum aye mean him ken di order, uderwun
           aye mean him gonna do it.

NED: Thus. Kill the dogs!

HITI: Aye, aye, sir!

NED: And when you've done it, show me your thumb,
           like this.

NED demonstrates a thumbs up.

           That means all is well.

HITI tries a thumbs up, but does it with both thumbs.

NED: We don't use both thumbs or we'd fall over the gunwale –

HITI: – one hand fe me, one hand for the ship.

NED: Good, you're learning. Both thumbs up is reserved for the most brilliant thing, the most fantastical event. Go on!

HITI: Aye, aye sir.

HITI runs off, but stops to stare at MATA. She walks down stage for direct address.

MATA: That's Hiti. He's only a boy. Fifteen. Watch what he does. *(Beat.)* He stares at me. He'll touch his dick in a minute, watch.

A couple of beats of staring from HITI and then he touches his dick.

These English sailors, their cocks are poxy. They are not circumcised. Urgh! And how can I describe their breath? You know what a dead shark's arse smells like? Yes? You, I'm talking to you. Yes. So it's about twice as bad as that. Why do we sleep with them then? For these.

Holds up a nail.

Nails. Girls, hands up, who would sleep with a sailor for a nail? Two nails? *(There's always one.)* Most of you ladies would say 'no'. But on my island there is no iron. A nail for us is a miracle, a piece of the sun. So the question you girls should ask yourselves is, 'would I have sex with a stranger for a piece of the sun'. Ah! One night I fell asleep on The Bounty with Ned Young. Titreano woke him and they went up on deck. I followed, silently, a few paces behind. I saw my Ned and Titreano, they did this together, they took their knives and they started cutting through the rope of the anchor, which is really thick, as thick as, an arm. You! Raise your arm.

16

She mime saws through the audience member's arm.

> And they sawed and sawed and when it was
> cut the rope slipped into the lagoon, and The
> Bounty started to drift and I saw that there was
> a boat ahead with men rowing and it was pulling
> us out of the reef towards the open sea. Yes, we
> were being stolen, like chickens, like goats,
> stolen away, our lives stolen, never to see Tahiti
> again.

NED: Hiti!

HITI: Aye, aye sir!

HITI runs off. NED exits.

TE'O: I'm starving. I could eat a whale.

MATA: So do we now eat separate from the men again,
            like on Tahiti.

FASTO: Yes! It is tapu!

TE'O: I like eating with the men, they're funny.

MI MITTI: We are Tahitian women, we don't eat with the
            men. It is tapu.

WALUA: We're not on Tahiti!

MI MITTI: We must not lose our traditions, or we lose
            ourselves.

FASTO: What are the rules?! It's so confusing!

WALUA: We're English now!

TE'O: Yes. We were four months on the ship. All our
            traditions are lost. We are no longer Tahitian.
            And I don't care. I like being English.

MI MITTI: No. A ship is only temporary but this is
            permanent, and we can restore our traditions,
            and live in the right way, here.

TE LAHU: No. We must return to Tahiti. We can do this, we
            have The Bounty.

17

FASTO:	Mi Mitti, your Queen is happy here. Don't speak to your Queen like that!
MI MITTI:	This island has everything.
TE LAHU:	Except my children.
MI MITTI:	You can have more children here. With Mister Brown.
TE LAHU:	You volunteered, to sail with Titreano. I didn't. I was stolen. What will be a home to you, will be a prison to me.
TE'O:	I didn't like Tahiti. It was all rules, rules, rules.
MATA:	And mosquitoes.
WALUA:	And we have white husbands, that's good isn't it? We'll have white children. Te'o is pregnant.
TE'O:	Yes, my blood hasn't come.

They make a fuss of TE'O.

TE LAHU:	For the sake of this unborn child. We must find a way back to Tahiti. For there can be no future here.
TE'O:	No! My baby is English.
MATA:	Why do you fear for the future?
TE LAHU:	During our journey here I watched Titreano.
MI MITTI:	You watched my husband?
TE LAHU:	He has lost his authority.
MI MITTI:	He sailed The Bounty, he found this island!
TE LAHU:	We all sailed the ship.
MI MITTI:	He read the charts.
WALUA:	Can you read their sea charts?
TE LAHU:	Of course not.
TE'O:	Stop farting out your mouth then.

They laugh.

TE LAHU: When McKoy shot that chief, the one that stole the jacket, at Purutea –

FASTO: – they are all thieves on Purutea.

MATA: We were outnumbered, we could have been torn limb from limb.

TE LAHU: But what did Christian do to punish McKoy? Lash him, beat him, kill him? No! He turned his back and walked away. Titreano has no authority. And a people without a leader will get lost.

TE'O: Alright, don't go on about it.

MATA: We can live here, but we need to know how to live.

WALUA: We're English now, we married them!

TE'O: Yes, and this is a part of England.

TE LAHU: On Tahiti Mi Mitti is Ra'atira, our Queen, on Tahiti. I am Arioi, I make performances, on Tahiti. And you are the Manuhane, the people, of Tahiti. But we are all cast away now, we are all nothing now. Prisoners, slaves, we are living in oblivion, at the edge of the world, divided from our people by the ocean, washed up on a lost island, like fish bones.

WALUA: I'm sick of listening to you, you whining turd.

MATA: Is this England or is this Tahiti.

TE'O: My man refuses to call me Te'o, he calls me Mary.

FASTO: He can't pronounce Te'o?

They laugh.

TE'O: Mary is the name of the English God's wife.

FASTO: What's the English god's name then?

TE'O:	God. Just God. Like that. God. He doesn't have a name. They just call him God.
MATA:	That's like having a boat and calling it Boat.
TE LAHU:	They lack imagination.
WALUA:	Quintal calls me Sarah. Which was his mother's name in England.
TE LAHU:	Did he used to fuck his mother then?

They laugh.

WALUA:	He calls me Sarah, because he loves me!
TE LAHU:	Oh mummy, mummy, Sarah, oh mummy, oh, oh, oh!

WALUA clips TE LAHU and they start fighting. Uproar. The others break it up.

WALUA:	At least I've got a proper man for a husband not a freak.
TE LAHU:	I didn't choose him.
WALUA:	What were you doing at the party then?
TE'O:	Collecting nails.

They laugh.

TE LAHU:	I was not collecting nails.
MATA:	You are Arioi, you were there to dance.
TE LAHU:	I was stolen.

They laugh.

TE LAHU:	*(To MI MITTI.)* You were married to Titreano on Tahiti. My question is, did you know their plans? Did you help them plan our abduction?
FASTO:	You cannot ask such a question of our Queen.
MATA:	Te Lahu is Arioi, that is her job, to ask strange questions.
TE'O:	Yes! Answer Te Lahu's question.

MI MITTI stands and walks away.

TE LAHU: Our Queen betrayed us.

FASTO is crying. NED enters and rings the bell.

FASTO: I hate it here. Everything is wrong!

TE LAHU: From this day Mi Mitti is not my Queen.

TE LAHU walks away from the group. NED rings the bell, politely. QUINTAL is by the bell singing and drinking.

NED: *(To QUINTAL.)* I said, no drinking.

QUINTAL: Go wipe your catastrophe, sir.

             (Singing.) Shanty man, oh! shanty man
             (Burps.)
             Who's got a birth for a shanty man.
             Sing you a song of a world gone wrong
             and we got no use for a shanty man

QUINTAL rings the bell manically. Singing as the men gather. NED Young, WILLIAM MCKOY, MATTHEW QUINTAL, WILLIAM BROWN, and JOHN ADAMS. Enter CHRISTIAN.

CHRISTIAN: Mammu! Mammu!

MCKOY: We havenae had our ration yet sir!

CHRISTIAN: Let us, as a priority, consider the future of the rum ration.

MCKOY: I vote to double it!

OTHERS   Hear, hear! / Aye!

CHRISTIAN: Half a pint a day for each man will last us but one year.

BROWN: And we are here forever.

QUINTAL: McKoy reckons he can distill, we got the copper out the ship.

MCKOY: I was apprenticed to a distillery as a bairn sir.

QUINTAL: He worked in the bottling shed, emptying bottles.

21

CHRISTIAN: I am hopeful that life here might offer alternatives to drunkeness as a distraction.

QUINTAL: I've had half a pint of rum, a pint of white wine and a quart of porter every day of my life since I was fourteen Mister Christian.

CHRISTIAN: Then I apologise to you personally Mister Quintal for having failed to discover an island blessed with a livery tavern.

BROWN: You've done very well finding this land Mister Christian, but I've seen the charts I don't think it's Pitcairn.

CHRISTIAN: The Admiralty have charted Pitcairn incorrectly.

The men know the importance of this and cheer loudly.

Yes! We are twenty-five two south and one hundred and thirty west. Captain Carteret was out by three degrees.

QUINTAL: What a wanker!

Further cheering.

CHRISTIAN: Three degrees is not invisible. We need to be constant in our vigil. If Bligh has made land –

QUINTAL: I should have blown the bugger's brains out.

ALL Aye / yeah / for sure / grumbles.

CHRISTIAN: So we keep a watch night and day from the heights. That was my last order. I shall no longer be burdened with the responsibility nor shall I claim its privileges. Our ranks are equal, I am henceforth, Fletcher Christian.

He takes his tunic off and drops it on the grass.

Mister Young? Where is your tunic?

NED: I have bequeathed my commission to the boy Hiti, your taio.

22

CHRISTIAN: Then we are levelled. I have made mistakes.
To consider the many deaths that it has taken
to get us to this peaceful place –

ADAMS: – who's died?

NED: The natives killed at Tubuai.

ADAMS: Think of them as animals sir, not men, that way
you won't grieve none.

CHRISTIAN: Pitcairn is now our purser.

QUINTAL: Let's hope she's no nip cheese!

CHRISTIAN: The land is fertile, the seas teem with fish, there
is fresh water. But that is not our only fortune.
How blessed are we to have the skills of the
very gardener that Sir Joseph Banks himself
chose for the breadfruit expedition, William
Brown of Leicester!

Applause/cheers.

MCKOY: Give that man a woman now!

CHRISTIAN: Bill McKoy. No British colony should want for a
Scot!

QUINTAL: You mean, no British colony should want for
Scotch.

CHRISTIAN: Bill McKoy may not be guild, but I have never
seen a finer white iron man!

Cheers.

CHRISTIAN: We have no books, but I'll wager Mister
Young has read any author you care to name.
His instruction will be our instruction.

Cheers.

Alexander Smith. Pitcairn is an island nation,
seamanship will be much in demand.

ADAMS: I am not Alexander Smith sir.

23

MCKOY:	Who are yee then man?
QUINTAL:	Oliver Cromwell.
ADAMS:	As it is writ in the parish, my name is John Adams.
QUINTAL:	You'll always be Reckless Jack to me.
NED:	Why did you sign as Alex Smith?
ADAMS:	My father, also John Adams, was pressed and then deserted a man o' war and took the meat with him, sir.

The men are giggling.

NED:	And signing with Bligh as John Adams might alert the Admiralty?
ADAMS:	I thought they might hang me by mistake.
MCKOY:	They'll hang yee as John Adams, Reckless Jack or Alex Smith.
QUINTAL:	Aye, they'll hang all three of you.
ADAMS:	I gave Bligh his breeches, to cover his modesty. He noted that.
QUINTAL:	I wish you had gone in the damned launch. I'd have a bigger garden and two wives.
CHRISTIAN:	Mammu! Mammu! Matthew Quintal. A seaman with a refreshing directness of manner. Without this man I could not have found the strength to take the ship.

Cheers.

CHRISTIAN:	We have all the essentials for this challenge.
NED:	Wait. You have not spoken of yourself.
BROWN:	Aye.
NED:	All successful nations boast a man of vision, whose disciplines can raise the common people above their instinctive predilection to savagery.

On this isle we shall want for culture, and those
of us that have been exposed to the refinements
of the opera, concerts –

QUINTAL: – you, you mean.

NED: Yes. I hope that as an expert observator of the
stars you might share that passion with us all.
The night sky is the only theatre we can attend.

CHRISTIAN: I shall. To govern ourselves we need a polity
that will serve *us* rather than King, Court,
or Church. The kelson of our society shall be
equality, founded on the love of our fellow man.
We have as yet not one edict written down, we
have only the natural law of men living in
extremis. Let our needs be our guide, and let
us eschew the sophistry of Europe. We need
a title for this parliament. Might I suggest,
'the court of Yarning'.

QUINTAL: 'Yarning?' Like telling a story?

MCKOY: Bligh lashed me fae yarning.

BLIGH: Bligh saw yarning as revolution. This our
yarning court is the Parliament of our revolution!

BROWN: These words sound rather grand to me sir and
I approve.

MCKOY: Do we take nae heed of God?

CHRISTIAN: It is as if we find ourselves at the beginning of
time. Man and Woman in a natural state. Let
Tahiti be our model where men live without a
sense of vice, without prejudices, without
disputes. Born under a beautiful sky, nourished
on the fruits of the earth which is fertile without
tillage, ruled by patriarchs rather than kings,
knowing no other god but love. There is no
equivalent paradise in Christendom.

QUINTAL: Amsterdam? 'Cept the women charge.

25

The men laugh. CHRISTIAN struggles on.

CHRISTIAN: We are men, that is enough, our moral sense is innate. We do not need God to be good.

NED: And if all else fails I have the Bounty Bible.

MCKOY: Do we's get to vote on everything?

CHRISTIAN: We are nine men in number, so we should never be locked.

QUINTAL: We ain't nine men.

MCKOY: We're six.

CHRISTIAN: Oha, Menalee and Hiti are men.

ADAMS: The Indians?

QUINTAL: Go wipe!

Uproar.

BROWN: The natives' skill in horticulture is superior to ours, they know how to fish these waters, and Oha, is my taio, my brother for life.

MCKOY: If you goes ahead and makes the natives equal sir –

CHRISTIAN: – it will not be my decision, the Yarning court, this meeting –

QUINTAL: – will they be given land?

CHRISTIAN: Naturally. The division of the island would be into nine parts.

Uproar.

QUINTAL: One of them's a damned boy!

MCKOY: He don't even have a woman.

QUINTAL: And who will work our land?

BROWN: The natives are free men, not slaves.

QUINTAL: You took them on to work the damned ship, not to be masters over us.

MCKOY: We can't divide the land nine ways, there's
            nae enough.

BROWN: You are presuming enclosure.

NED: It would be a very English comedy to see the
            garden of Eden sprouting fences.

BROWN: The pigs can run wild, like us, they have
            nowhere to go. And we could consider the
            island common land, and work it equally.

ADAMS: No. I want my a plot of land, and I'll fence it off,
            and I'll put my damned name on it.

QUINTAL: Which name are you gonna use?

Laughter.

NED: Let's vote.

MCKOY: What are we voting on?

CHRISTIAN: The proposal is that the three Indian men will be
            equal yarners with equal land rights, each man
            taking one ninth part of Pitcairn. All those in
            favour of this proposition raise your hand.

CHRISTIAN raises, as does BROWN. No one else. There is laughter.

CHRISTIAN: Ned, Menalee is your taio, that means he is your
            brother. Is your brother not your equal?

QUINTAL: I don't have a taio. I think that's all Tahitian arse
            wipe.

CHRISTIAN: *(Fired up.)* We came south for the breadfruit,
            cheap food, to perpetuate and make more
            profitable a serfdom which we would disavow
            within an English shire but which we allow to
            flourish in the Americas.

QUINTAL: What's he on about?

BROWN: Slavery.

CHRISTIAN: We can manumise these men. If they are free we
            are free. We will vote again tomorrow.

27

MCKOY: Until ye gets yer preferred result!?

CHRISTIAN: This is too important!

NED: We need to decide the fate of the Bounty.

QUINTAL: She's gotta burn! Damn it! If the navy find the island, they'll see her. If she ain't there, they'll pass on, as there is no natural landing.

MCKOY: And they wouldnae expect us to burn her.

BROWN: Because that would be madness. I'm not a mutineer, so I do not fear the navy.

QUINTAL: They'll hang you Brown, not for mutiny, but for knowing me.

BROWN: After a year or so, we might feel the need to explore. There may be a plant, or tree we need. I think we should keep her.

Enter TE LAHU from upstage. She stands some way off and listens.

MCKOY: Hey, look, that Te Lahu's listening to us. She's trouble.

QUINTAL: I'll knock some sense into her later.

Laughter.

NED: John Adams?

ADAMS: I ain't got nothing to fear from the Admiralty. I'd keep her.

NED: If the navy find Pitcairn they'll come ashore for water. Ship or no ship. And as a gentleman I quite like having my own ship.

CHRISTIAN: This island will satisfy all our wants but one.

MCKOY: Whisky?

CHRISTIAN: We do not have sufficient women.

ADAMS: One each is enough.

QUINTAL: Speak for yourself.

CHRISTIAN: Hiti will need a wife.

QUINTAL: His balls ain't dropped.

CHRISTIAN: An island, which for us is a paradise, will
             become for him a prison.

QUINTAL: We can't risk our necks so's some Indian kid can
           have a tumble.

CHRISTIAN's head drops.

CHRISTIAN: Within two months we visit Tahiti and invite
             further female volunteers.

NED: Why such specific timing?

CHRISTIAN: I set Bligh adrift on the twenty-eighth of April
             1789, nine months ago. My calculations are that
             if he has made land –

MCKOY: – Bligh is fish food.

CHRISTIAN: – I know Bligh and I promise you, he lives!
             The earliest a navy Man O'War will dock in
             Tahiti will be one year from that day. That gives
             us three months.

QUINTAL: That ship must burn, it's as good as a pin in the
           Admiralty map!

MCKOY: Burn her!

NED: The proposal is 'we retain the Bounty'.
       All in favour?

CHRISTIAN, BROWN, ADAMS and NED raise their hands.

NED: That she should burn?

MCKOY and QUINTAL raise their hands.

NED: The vote is four to two, we retain the ship.

QUINTAL: No! My damned neck is at stake!
           (Re BROWN.) He won't swing! And he won't
           swing, so's why does they get a vote?

CHRISTIAN: Because he is a fellow Yarner!

29

QUINTAL: Damn your Yarning court!

Enter HITI, still wearing his newly acquired tunic which is now covered in blood.

BROWN: My God, the boy is injured! What is it?

QUINTAL: He ain't injured.

MCKOY: What blood is this yer little devil?

HITI looks to NED. QUINTAL sees this, and looks to NED, and then CHRISTIAN.

QUINTAL: Shhhh! Quiet! Listen.

They listen to the silence.

QUINTAL: The dogs. They're not barking. The little
                   bugger's killed the dogs. Have you killed
                  my dog?

HITI: Aye, aye, sir.

QUINTAL: Who told you to kill my dog?

HITI: Mister Young tell him me, Titreano tell him
            Mister Young.

QUINTAL looks at CHRISTIAN.

QUINTAL: You told him to kill my dog?

QUINTAL goes to the fire pit and takes a burning stick, and heads off down stage right.

MCKOY: Yer didnae trust us to vote the right way on the
            dogs then Mister Christian. Eh?

MCKOY goes to the fire and he too picks out a burning stick, and heads down to the Bounty.

CHRISTIAN: Rather I had no faith in my power to persuade you.

NED: We can stop them!

CHRISTIAN: Today possibly. Tomorrow?

NED: If they burn the Bounty this island is a prison.

CHRISTIAN: And our sentence a life sentence.

The remaining mutineers walk down stage and watch the Bounty burn.
The light fades and the glow of the burning Bounty dominates. They are
joined by the women and the native men, all lit by the burning Bounty.
Some of the women cry. HITI steps down stage for direct address.

End of scene.

ACT 2
SCENE 1

The Bounty burning at night, segues into a new morning.

HITI: *(Direct address.)* Everybody did nothing, only
               watching. The women crying watch, the men sit
               holding their heads in their hands like stones,
               and watch. Me, Hiti, Midshipman, I didn't
               watch, I ran down the path screaming, 'that is
               my ship, my English navy ship, don't burn my
               ship!' But Mister Quintal he punched me in the
               mouth. That shut me up double quick. I lost one
               tooth and one tooth is now wobbly. This one,
               can you see, it is loose. I can't eat meat on this
               side. Only fruit this side, meat the other. My
               mother had a saying 'good days are life, bad
               days are history'. And this story I tell you today
               is the history, not the life, I don't do every day,
               that would send you to sleep, which would be
               dangerous because some of you are standing
               up, so the next bad day, the next history day,
               is today, one year later. I was collecting crayfish,
               they're easy to catch, and fat, you just have to be
               quick, and I am quick. Like that. See. That's
               quick. And I am standing in a rock pool, staring
               into the water, a wave will make the water
               bubble, and you stand still wait for it to calm.
               When the water cleared I saw the face of a
               woman staring at me. And I was so scared I
               couldn't scream, just opened my mouth like this,
               oh, oh, oh, and my mouth like this, oh, oh, oh.
               And the water around my knees is blood. She is
               dead.

31

Women screaming. HITI runs up to the eyrie where CHRISTIAN is staring out to sea. Enter OHA carrying the wet and bloody body of Paurai. She wears good leather English boots. Enter NED.

NED: John Adams' wife?

OHA: Eeyeuh!

TE'O: Paurai! She's dead.

Enter TE LAHU.

TE LAHU: At last she has stopped crying.

Enter CHRISTIAN and everyone except ADAMS and MCKOY.

NED: Adams' wife.

CHRISTIAN: Where did you find her?

OHA: Hiti him see her down ted side.

MENALEE: She was crying all day long today.

TE LAHU: She cried all day every day.

QUINTAL: English!

CHRISTIAN: She must have slipped collecting eggs.

NED: Or leapt.

TE'O: Na! Es storle. Her no leap leap!

QUINTAL: Pushed?

CHRISTIAN: We must cancel today's yarning.

NED: Hiti. Get Mister Adams.

HITI goes off. MCKOY arrives.

MCKOY: Paurai? Adams was sick of her. The wee lass was
            always bawling.

CHRISTIAN: This is not the time for speculation. Mister
            Adams does not know she's dead.

BROWN: He knows she's dead.

CHRISTIAN: Why do you say that?

32

BROWN: Because he's not here.

Enter ADAMS and HITI.

ADAMS: *(Beat.)* Them's my boots. Give 'em here.

HITI takes her boots off and gives them to ADAMS.

> We got a yarning at midday, to talk about the hole in my fence. I say we meet now, we're all here. And we can add to the business some talk about which woman I'm gonna be getting now that this one's dead.

ADAMS walks to the log and sits. The women take Paurai's body away.

CHRISTIAN: It doesn't seem right.

MCKOY: We's all here now.

QUINTAL: I wanna know if Reckless Jack pushed her off!

ADAMS squares up to QUINTAL.

QUINTAL: Come on then. I'll rip your head off and shit down your neck.

BROWN: Let us yarn, like gentlemen.

NED: The business today was to be the dispute between Mister Christian and Mister Adams over a fence. However, the tragic events –

ADAMS: – I'm not letting up on my fence on account of the death of an Indian.

BROWN: Your wife.

Some laugh.

ADAMS: I can't go another day with an 'ole in my fence.

QUINTAL: Did you push her?

NED: It is alleged that Mister Christian threatened to shoot Mister Adams' sow.

CHRISTIAN: If his sow were to break through the fence and on to my crops, yes.

33

QUINTAL: *(Prodding ADAMS.)* You pushed her didn't you?

NED: Whose fence is it?

ADAMS: The fence is mine, the hole is his.

Laughter.

NED: *(To ADAMS.)* Why don't you mend the fence?

ADAMS: My fence ain't the problem, the problem's his hole.

Laughter.

NED: Mister Christian, is it your hole?

CHRISTIAN: My goat made the hole.

QUINTAL: So it's your goat's hole?

Laughter.

CHRISTIAN: My goat made a hole in his fence, yes.

NED: Ergo the hole is your responsibility. Surely it is your task to repair it?

ADAMS: If he touches my fence I'll kill him!

Laughter.

CHRISTIAN: This is the nub! On Tubuai I had this man clapped in irons for whoring ashore contrary to my orders. He has never forgiven me that. Adams raised a musket at me, over his fence.

NED: Did you threaten Mister Christian with a musket?

ADAMS: Aye, I did and I'll do it again, if his goat comes through that hole he tutored her to make.

BROWN: *(To ADAMS.)* Why do you not splice the hole?

ADAMS: I'll mend his hole but I want a consideration for the labour.

NED: Ah! Your price?

ADAMS: I want for candlenuts.

NED: *(To CHRISTIAN.)* A basket of candlenuts?

34

QUINTAL: Or he'll shove you off the cliff.

CHRISTIAN: Agreed.

NED: *(Writing.)* And recorded. The second item of business.

ADAMS: I can't live here without a woman.

QUINTAL: If it's a woman you want, go to Nottingham.

CHRISTIAN: What a different situation this might be if we had a two hundred and fifteen ton schooner which could reach Tahiti in a month.

MCKOY: Why disnae Reckless Jack take Fasto off Oha?

CHRISTIAN: Because Oha is a man not a beast!

MCKOY: Aye, but Oha spends all day on the mooch.

QUINTAL: You got to start him to get him on his feet.

CHRISTIAN: You whip Oha?

MCKOY: Every time you turn around the man's back on his arse.

CHRISTIAN: Oha is high born, he's a chief!

MCKOY: Aye, that's why you have to start him.

NED: Mister Brown, can you apply your intellect to this conundrumical dilemma.

BROWN: If Mister Adams were given Te'o's daughter, Scully –

ADAMS: – she's a year old!

QUINTAL: She'll be on the reds by thirteen, if not afore.

MCKOY: Yous'll have tae beat your meat for thirteen years man!

Laughter.

QUINTAL: I know Reckless Jack, you won't agree to that, you're a right mutton monger, ain't yer.

ADAMS: I want Mareva or Fasto. I prefer the look of Fasto.

35

QUINTAL: All cats are grey, when the candle's out.

CHRISTIAN: Mareva is married to Menalee and Fasto to Oha. They both have husbands!

ADAMS: Ask them two girls what they want. I'll wager they choose an Englishman over a slave any day of the week.

CHRISTIAN: So if Fasto is given to Adams then Mareva has to whore herself to three men?

QUINTAL: Aye, that could work.

MCKOY: It's nae hardship for them Indians to share a woman.

ADAMS: And I'm Christian ain't I. God said go forth and multiply. I can't do that on me own now can I?

BROWN: The two native marriages have not produced children. Mister Christian has a child, Quintal a son, and McKoy's woman is carrying again.

NED: Are you saying that the native couplings will ever be barren?

BROWN: These girls can volunteer a miscarriage through violent massage. There is no desire, within the native women who are married to native men, to produce.

CHRISTIAN: *Because* the child will be born a slave!

ADAMS: Aye, that's my point.

NED: *(To BROWN.)* Mister Brown, what population do you think our island can sustain?

BROWN: Many many more than we. Perhaps ten fold.

NED: Who is your preferred wife?

ADAMS: Either of them'll do.

QUINTAL: Damn you! I thought it was love!

NED: Might I suggest we draw straws.

CHRISTIAN: *(Exasperated.)* The drawing of straws?! For a woman?!

NED: It will avoid covetousness, a good thing in God's eyes.

NED picks two straws.

Fasto, the short straw. Mareva, the long straw.

QUINTAL: You got them the wrong way round.

NED: Choose John.

ADAMS chooses.

NED: The short straw. Fasto.

QUINTAL: Woo! Lucky girl.

NED: Fasto. Step forward!

CHRISTIAN: I'm disgusted.

CHRISTIAN exits to his eyrie. MI MITTI follows. FASTO and OHA step forward.

NED: Fasto. The Yarning court has decided that you are to be wife to Mister Adams.

FASTO takes a step forward, almost keen, but is held by OHA.

OHA: Ay es ra'atira! Chief! No man tek woman fe me disday!

QUINTAL raises his musket at OHA.

QUINTAL: Let that girl go or I'll blow your damned brains into the ocean.

OHA assesses his situation. MCKOY draws a knife. He lets FASTO go. She skips to ADAMS.

ADAMS: Stand behind me girl.

OHA: Ay es ra'atira no manuhane! Ay no born fe dig dig yoo groun!

OHA turns and runs into the woods. The situation relaxes.

NED: *(Standing.)* McKoy, do we have any leg irons remaining? Or have you formed them all into hoes?

MCKOY: I'm working on them now.

NED: Then stop the work. I fear, we're going to need them for their original purpose.

End of scene.

ACT 2
SCENE 2

Up in the eyrie cave. CHRISTIAN is standing, keenly looking through the telescope. His log book is beside him.

MI MITTI: Titreano, my husband, are you crazy?!

CHRISTIAN: I voted against!

MI MITTI: This yarning yarning! What are you always talking about? In England, does King Toote have one vote and all the English manuhane have another one vote?

CHRISTIAN: Another vote. Not another one vote. And don't repeat words. We wouldn't say yarning yarning or siki siki.

MI MITTI: I am not learning English now, I am asking you what kind of chief you are?

CHRISTIAN: To answer your question. In England Captain Cook would have a vote, yes, and the English people would not. So, in that regard, Pitcairn is in advance of England. And I am proud of that.

MI MITTI: What are you looking for with the telescope? You have trouble here today, and you are looking out to sea.

CHRISTIAN: I thought I saw a ship.

MI MITTI: There is no ship, there will be no ship, we are nowhere. Your heart is in England.

CHRISTIAN: I think about my mother, and the pain that my actions must have brought her. You understand the importance of honour.

MI MITTI: Your mother in England will not die with a knife across her throat. Your wife on Pitcairn might. You must be a big man now, and kill Oha.

CHRISTIAN: I cannot kill men that have done me no wrong!

MI MITTI: Oha will have to kill you! You took his woman away. You must kill him first! Why did you not kill Captain Bligh? Have I married a little man!?

She is gone, descending. CHRISTIAN looks on. She passes NED ascending.

NED: I sent Menalee after Oha. He might take the canoe. I am proposing that we burn it.

CHRISTIAN: Why not? Burning is established as the solution to all problems.

NED: We could let him take, he'd die at sea, and that would solve one problem.

CHRISTIAN: We need the canoe.

NED: You should've seen Fasto take the hand of Adams? Keen! Adams, a common man to her is the conjunction of Apollo and Achilles.

CHRISTIAN: We are all gods in their eyes.

NED: Add to this the natural licentiousness of their women.

CHRISTIAN: The marriages of the men and their chosen women have been recognised. That should decrease the incidence of venereals.

NED: But increase the incidence of adultery.

CHRISTIAN: Is there adultery?

NED: All the men find Mi Mitti attractive –

CHRISTIAN: – My wife!

NED: – but Quintal presses.

39

CHRISTIAN: He wouldn't dare.

NED: He understands that Mi Mitti is ra'atira.
He knows her only choice –

CHRISTIAN: – was between you or I.

NED: Yet Quintal is uniquely excited by, what might
be called, the general levelling.

CHRISTIAN: Thank you my friend. I will bear it in mind.

NED: You had promised to enthrall me with the
theatre of the stars.

NED turns a page in CHRISTIAN's star log.

CHRISTIAN: You will see no ascent of Venus, here, or in
your lifetime. They arrive in pairs, eight years
apart, but separated by one hundred and twenty
years. It's a rare entertainment.

NED: With an extravagant interval. I wouldn't wait for
the second act.

CHRISTIAN: Venus is not the only show in town.
My calculations promise a total eclipse of the
sun. And it's not all amusement Ned, my
calendar is sound and I can now divine the
position of each planet and the moon to a
specific day.

NED: I'm impressed.

CHRISTIAN: Reason. Muster the men.

NED descends. HITI arrives.

HITI: Titreano! Es storle? Yoo tek wife off fe Oha?

CHRISTIAN: The yarning court made a decision, not I.

HITI: Him chief semuz King Toote!

CHRISTIAN: Hiti, have you seen Quintal talking to my wife?

HITI: Aye, wan time an unuduwan time.

CHRISTIAN: I want you to tell me if he approaches her. And what is her reaction.

HITI: Ay gwen in dem wood wid di long eye.

CHRISTIAN: No! I am not asking you to spy on them. Just let me know if they speak. Go on then, off you go.

HITI doesn't move.

What is it?

HITI: Ay wan woman.

CHRISTIAN: You're too young.

HITI: No! Wan dawn, uderwan dawn, ha unuderwan dawn.

CHRISTIAN: Every dawn, yes, what do you do every dawn?

HITI: Ay hide me in di big one iron tree yonder, down ted side.

CHRISTIAN: I know it. Where the women bathe.

HITI: Aye, aye! Owuz women no ken ay is in di tree.

CHRISTIAN: You hide? They don't know you're in the tree.

HITI: Eeyeuh! Ay see dem. Me feelin' big fe Mata in me heart.

CHRISTIAN: Hiti, some advice. Mata is very pretty, yes. And she is Ned's wife. And don't try and grow up too quickly, you might not like it when you do.

End of scene.

ACT 2
SCENE 3

OHA and MENALEE in the woods hiding.

OHA: Don't look at me. You should not even look at me. I am ra'atira, a chief, high born. You are manuhane, you should not be able to speak

41

to me even. And yet I have had to share a
woman with you, a manuhane.

MENALEE: Yes, that must be very difficult for you. But it is a
great honour for me.

OHA: Everything is different here. But I must have a wife!

MENALEE: Yes! You're a chief. You can have any woman
you choose. Titreano has deceived you. His
promises to you of land, and wealth are like the
wind.

OHA: On Tubuai I had many women.

MENALEE: He makes you work the land. Which is stupid.
Stupid because you've never worked, and you're
all fat, which is how it should be. Your job is to
eat.

OHA: Every night since I was thirteen I have had a
woman. One night I had seven women. All
sisters. Ah, yes. A great great night.

MENALEE: Titreano has made the manuhane ra'atira,
nd the ra'atira manuhane. I don't understand
why anyone would want to turn the world
upside down.

OHA: Night is day, and day is night.

MENALEE: I left Tahiti because he promised me my own
farm. And when we arrived here my heart lifted.

OHA: You're a farmer, you understand the soil. I don't.

MENALEE: No, you're useless.

OHA: Useless?

MENALEE: I mean, you're not a farmer, and I have to do
half your work.

OHA: The land would be easier to work if it was mine.

MENALEE: I'm a slave twice over. Once to them and again
to you. Which is a great honour.

OHA: I have a plan.

MENALEE: Take the canoe?

OHA: Why leave such a plentiful island? With so many women.

MENALEE: Ah! Kill the English?

OHA: There are enough women here for me to live like a chief, and you would have Mareva for yourself.

MENALEE: But I cannot kill Ned Young. He is my taio.

OHA: Taio! He cannot be your taio, he's not one of us.

MENALEE: I can't kill my taio. I could kill the others, and you kill my taio!?

OHA: So be it.

MENALEE: We have no muskets.

OHA: You, walk into the village and take a musket, and bring it to me. Say you are going hunting for a pig.

MENALEE: Very clever. Good! Tomorrow I will say that I need a musket to hunt a pig.

OHA grabs him, shakes him.

OHA: You are hunting pigs for me *today*!

MENALEE: Today?

OHA: Today!

MENALEE: Today!

MENALEE bows before OHA, and exits.

End of scene.

ACT 2
SCENE 4

NED YOUNG is on BROWN's ground. BROWN is working sorting cuttings.

43

NED:	Look at this! William, you have turned the Garden of Eden into… Norwich.
BROWN:	What do you want Ned Young?
NED:	Does Pitcairn have yeast?
BROWN:	McKoy begs me for yeast every day for his distillery. He's using a sugar beet mash and failing with it.
NED:	For want of yeast?
BROWN:	Yeast and an education.
NED:	I am not in league with those two.
BROWN:	Do you have your own distillery?
NED:	Look man! Pitcairn's yeast is not your yeast.
BROWN:	It is, and I am its jailor. To have Quintal and McKoy unfettered with an endless supply of alcohol would be suicide for us all.
NED:	I am ill. I need yeast for an essay at a cure.
BROWN:	I don't believe you.
NED:	My father considered it to be a blight in my African blood. Mata found me on the floor, faint.
BROWN:	I know of no medicines that depend on yeast.
NED:	You will not hoard power on this island! We, are all levelled, thus your knowledge is my knowledge. And, my life is at stake!
BROWN:	Your life?
NED:	Aye, my life.
BROWN:	Do you swear to keep the knowledge from McKoy?
NED:	I do.
BROWN:	*(Beat.)* The root of the ti tree.
NED:	Thank you.

NED turns and leaves.

You're a feculent beast aren't you Brown. Ugly
as sin itself. In the whole of your life you
couldn't get a woman to even look at you, until
you beached on Tahiti. Whence you filled
your boots. For six months. I watched you.
Lucifer in a permanent tumble. Pitiful.

End of scene.

ACT 2
SCENE 5

MATA direct address, but with TE LAHU preparing to dance.

MATA:　　Te Lahu is Arioi. Arioi are human, not god, but
special. On Tahiti we carry the Arioi about the
place, so that they don't have to touch the floor.
On Tahiti Arioi nail clippings, hair and shit is
sacred. The Arioi live in bands of about fifteen
to twenty men and women and their job is to
give surprises from village to village and we
must feed them, for they are not allowed to
work. Do you have this in England? Performers
who don't work in the fields, and the workers
have an obligation to feed them if they do
performances? You do? What are they called?
On Tahiti the men of the Arioi they can make
you laugh with just their penises. They pull
the skin and their two stones about to make
shapes, like a canoe, then like a dog, or two
chickens. One Arioi I saw made his penis
look like an old man with no teeth. It stayed
with me for many days. Most of the Arioi
surprises are about sex. My favourite surprise
is called 'fishing'. There is a short bit about
fishing at the beginning but very quickly
everyone is having sex in the boat, and there is
no more fishing after that. I have seen Te Lahu
perform the fishing surprise, and she was
brilliant. At the end she had two men in her,

one in the front hole, and one in the back hole,
and they lift her off the ground and carry her
into a canoe. No hands! Ha, ha! Yes! It was
really funny and everyone laughed. Te Lahu is
the only Arioi on Pitcairn so she performs her
surprises alone. I think we're ready to start.

TE LAHU performs her dance. Essentially it illustrates OHA's predicament, once a chief now a slave, being beaten, to the ground, gets up, beaten to the ground, gets up, beaten to the ground, gets up, beaten to the ground. And then sharpening his axe ready to kill his oppressors. The women gather and join in with the chorus. MENALEE provides percussion.

TE LAHU: *(In Tahitian.)* Why does the black man sharpen
his axe?
Why does the black man sharpen his axe?
To kill the white man,
to kill the white man

ALL WOMEN: *(In Tahitian.)* Why does the black man sharpen
his axe?
Why does the black man sharpen his axe?
To kill the white man,
to kill the white man

CHRISTIAN: Mi Mitti, translate for me please.

MI MITTI: Why does the black man sharpen his axe, to kill
the white man, to kill the white man.

She walks away. He ponders, then rings the bell. Enter MCKOY.

CHRISTIAN: McKoy! Manacles! Bring your musket too!

MCKOY: Aye, aye, sir.

MCKOY heads off. QUINTAL and ADAMS arrive.

QUINTAL: What is it? A ship?

CHRISTIAN: No! Quintal, Adams, arrest Menalee and Hiti.

QUINTAL: Aye, aye sir.

QUINTAL exits. ADAMS drags MENALEE over. Enter MCKOY with manacles which he strings around the tree.

ADAMS: We got to kill all the native men now.

CHRISTIAN: We'll do no such thing! You'll take direction from me!

ADAMS: By whose authority.

CHRISTIAN: Necessity itself!

Enter QUINTAL abusing HITI.

QUINTAL: Go on, you dog, move!

CHRISTIAN: Fetter them!

QUINTAL: Aye, aye sir.

CHRISTIAN: Ned, keep the women back.

QUINTAL: *(To TE LAHU.)* Oi! Stand off!

QUINTAL clips TE LAHU round the ear.

CHRISTIAN: McKoy! Get these women back!

MCKOY: Aye, aye sir!

MCKOY shoos back the women who stay and watch. MI MITTI stays watching CHRISTIAN and he plays to her, to prove his leadership.

CHRISTIAN: Menalee!? Does Oha have a musket?

MENALEE: Ay no bin see no musket wid him.

HITI: Titreano mi taio! Yoo no ka kill me! Mi taoi!

CHRISTIAN: I will not let you be harmed. *(To MENALEE.)* Where is Oha?

MENALEE: Kah wah!

QUINTAL kicks him in the groin.

QUINTAL: Speak the truth you damned dog!

CHRISTIAN: How do you know he has no musket? You must have spoken with him. Where is he hiding?

QUINTAL punches him. CHRISTIAN seems happy with that.

NED: Menalee, you may be my taio, and I love you like a brother, but if you are in league with Oha I will kill you myself.

MENALEE: Him yonder ted side. Him wan me join him. Fetch him muskets.

MCKOY: We got to kill these two now sir, then we form a vigilante and hunt down the black laird.

CHRISTIAN: *(To MENALEE.)* No. Release Menalee.

BROWN: Aye, aye.

WILLIAMS releases MENALEE.

CHRISTIAN: Menalee, this is a test of your loyalty. The prize is your life. Take this bowie knife, this musket –

Objections from the men.

– he has no lead, it is not a threat to us. Offer up the musket to Oha, take him some food, as a deception, as proof of your friendship. And when his guard is dropped, kill him.

QUINTAL: Oh aye, I like this!

MENALEE: Ay tek him musket an' wickles. Him turn back. I kill him bignayf.

CHRISTIAN: But! If the sun sinks behind the hill, and you have not returned with word that the task is completed, I will kill the boy Hiti.

HITI: Mi am yous taio Titreano!

NED: How do we know he's killed Oha?

CHRISTIAN: Menalee is a man of his word.

MENALEE: Ay gwen do dis fe yoo Titreano.

QUINTAL: Don't lie you devil, you'll do this 'cause you love your own life.

MENALEE is freed. He turns to go.

NED: *(Playing to MI MITTI.)* Wait! When you return, having killed Oha, deliver your word to Mister Christian, for you are a man of your word, but deliver Oha's head to me.

MENALEE: Him tete?

NED: As proof of the task completed.

ADAMS: And his hands. To be sure.

QUINTAL: Damn your blood Adams! We don't need his hands, we'll have his head!

NED: Go!

MENALEE exits.

CHRISTIAN: We muster again at sunset. Back to your houses, lock your doors, secure your muskets.

The men disperse. Except ADAMS and NED. CHRISTIAN exits to his eyrie.

NED: *(To ADAMS.)* You've started a war John Adams.

ADAMS: Some folk take things the wrong way.

HITI: Please sir! Some water.

NED: Of course.

NED goes to fetch water.

HITI: Will dem kill me?

NED: I'll not let them.

MI MITTI walks past NED. NED looks after her. She makes eye contact. HITI sees this.

NED: Mi Mitti? I would counsel against bathing whilst Oha is at large. It is not safe. Go home. Let your husband protect you.

MI MITTI: My husband is not at home.

MI MITTI exits. HITI and NED watch her go. After a pause, NED follows.

End of scene.

ACT 2
SCENE 6

MENALEE in the woods.

MENALEE: Chief Oha! It is me! Menalee!! I have brought you some food!

OHA appears with a musket raised pointing at MENALEE.

You've got a musket?!

OHA: I stole it from Mister Brown's house.

MENALEE: Good! So now we have two muskets. I have an axe too.

OHA: Why would they give you a musket and an axe?

MENALEE: They're crazy. The musket is to kill you and the axe is to chop off your head. Don't worry, I'm not going to. I've got some food here.

OHA: Do you have any meat? There is fruit out here, but no meat.

MENALEE: I've got plenty of meat. Ha! They gave me that as well!

OHA: Where is Hiti?

MENALEE: Hiti will join us after dark. By tomorrow we will have three muskets.

OHA: Tomorrow will be a great day.

MENALEE: Let us eat.

OHA: Were you followed?

MENALEE: No, no, they are stupid men. They didn't think of following me.

OHA: Come, I have a place to hide, it is shaded and we can eat and sleep.

OHA turns his back and walks off. MENALEE pauses, and then follows him.

End of scene.

ACT 2
SCENE 7

MI MITTI and NED.

NED: I was concerned for your safety.

MI MITTI: I don't believe you.

NED: What other motivation could I have?

MI MITTI: You're a man.

NED: And you are married, to my leader.

MI MITTI: You remember. You have a wife.

NED: Mata is young, yes, and pretty but she is manuhane

NED sits, invites her to join him.

MI MITTI: I can't sit with you.

NED: Au contraire. You can sit with me. You sat with
Captain Cook, you told me that once.

MI MITTI: King Toote was ra'atira.

NED: Captain Cook was manuhane. He became
ra'atira, through learning and position.

MI MITTI: Born manuhane, die manuhane. Born ra'atira,
die ra'atira.

NED: Not in England. Your husband is a perfect
example of this phenomenon, but in reverse.
Titreano, was born aristocracy, ra'atira, but, as
you know, became manuhane. His brother
played ducks and drakes with the family fortune.

MI MITTI: What is ducks and drakes?

NED: When you throw pebbles across the water and
they bounce, and sink, forever.

MI MITTI: Titreano brother threw their money into the sea?

NED: Metaphorically. In truth drink and gambling.
Has he not told you this? Their family have

nothing. Even I have more. My inheritance on St. Kitts is intact. A sugar plantation ten times the size of this island.

MI MITTI: So Titreano has lied to me?

NED: Omitted to mention.

MI MITTI stands, distressed.

What is it?

MI MITTI: I cannot sleep with manuhane.

MI MITTI turns to leave. NED stands.

NED: I thought you knew. I feel terrible, as if I have betrayed a confidentiality. I beg you, say nothing of this to him.

MI MITTI runs off.

End of scene.

ACT 2
SCENE 8

HITI is manacled.

HITI: Will this history day be the last day of my life? I had never thought one could see the sun move, it moves so slowly, taking twelve hours to get from there to there. Often I watched the sun and it doesn't move, you take your eyes off it and make play or work, and then you look back and it has moved, but never when you look at it. The sun always waits until you turn your back. And then it skips across the sky like a mouse. But that day I looked at the sun and I could see it moving, slowly yes, slowly, but moving, moving towards night and the end of my life.

Enter MATA.

MATA: Hiti? Water?

HITI: Please! Yes!

She gives him water and walks off.

HITI: Did you see that?! She gave me water! Why did
               she give me water? If she hated me she would
               not give me water. So at least she doesn't hate
               me. And she called me Hiti. By name. I think
               she did. Did she?! Oh my God, she must love
               me! I love her name, her full name is Mataohu.
               I love to say it. Mataohu.

*Enter CHRISTIAN. He looks at the sun. He rings the bell. Others begin
to gather.*

HITI: No kill me! Titreano. Ay bin di best damned
               good Midshipman. Yoo kah kill me, ay yoo taoi!

The sun goes down over the hill.

CHRISTIAN: I am fully aware of my social obligations as your
             taio. Onerous.

One by one people gather. QUINTAL puts a knife under HITI's chin.

QUINTAL: How do you want to die yer little Snacker? Knife
             or lead?

HITI: Lead. Yoo be quick.

MCKOY: We'll waste nae lead on a little devil like you.

QUINTAL: Can we burn him?

MCKOY: Aye, I ain't never seen a man burn.

QUINTAL: We lack for sport.

CHRISTIAN: Whatever we do with the wretch it will not be
             for your amusement.

Enter MENALEE carrying OHA's head by the hair. Everyone gathers.

HITI: Aaaaaaghhh!

QUINTAL inspects the head.

QUINTAL: It's definitely Oha's head. I reckon the chief is
             dead sir.

Laughter. MENALEE approaches CHRISTIAN still holding the head by the hair.

MENALEE: Titreano! Yoo see!? Ay es servant to yoo.
            Semuz brother!

CHRISTIAN: Out of my sight!

NED: Good work Menalee.

CHRISTIAN: McKoy! Release the boy!

MCKOY releases HITI. He runs to CHRISTIAN and hugs him. MENALEE turns to NED, approaches him. He puts the head on the ground before him.

MENALEE: Mister Young. Yoo mek me fetch him head.

NED: I commissioned this horror in the service of
            society in the hope that it will furnish us with
            a lasting peace.

CHRISTIAN: Go now, back to your labours, gather your wives
            and children and sleep peacefully knowing that
            there is no further threat to you.

The people disperse. CHRISTIAN turns to make the long ascent to his eyrie, as he does so he turns to MI MITTI, who turns her back on him. CHRISTIAN walks up the eyrie. MI MITTI approaches NED. NED grabs her hand. They kiss. CHRISTIAN does not see this. HITI does.

End of scene.

INTERVAL

ACT 3
SCENE 1

The women meet on the yarning log. TE LAHU, FASTO, TE'O, WALUA, MATA, and FASTO. MI MITTI is not there. They are animated. FASTO is being comforted. They are speaking Tahitian.

MATA: *(Direct address.)* Tahitian people, we like eating,
            and so we have a lot of fat people, and we
            like surfing, but our favourite thing is sex.
            We have sex everywhere, on the beach, outside,
            on the roof, and we don't care if anyone is

watching. If people start throwing things then we
might say something but that never happens.
Young people go into the hills in a big group
for days and do nothing but have sex with each
other. It is a good way to make friends. Do you
do that? And we have mahu. The Mahu are
men but dress as women, talk like women
and walk like women. They can tuck their penis
inside themselves, make it disappear, look more
like a woman. Do you have mahu? On Tahiti
a wife can sleep with her husband's brothers
and also his taio, and his honoured guests. Taio
means best friend. Do you do that in England?
It is good, but you have to be careful who you
marry, and if you're clever you sleep with all
the brothers first. Yes, we love sex, but one thing
we don't allow is rape.

FASTO: *(Crying.)* Quintal –

WALUA: – my husband, what did he do to you?

FASTO: – He found me collecting birds eggs, on the
            cliffs, and he forced me.

TE LAHU: He raped you?

FASTO: Yes.

Uproar.

TE LAHU: Mammu! Mammu!

WALUA: What did you do, show him your tits!?

TE LAHU: Mammu! Mammu!

FASTO: Rape is tapu.

TE LAHU: On Tahiti it is punishable by death.

WALUA: Or you can give meat to the family.

FASTO: No! It is always death!

Uproar.

MATA:	*(To WALUA.)* Fasto is not alone. Your man has forced me three times.
WALUA:	You!? You horny bitch. I don't believe it.
TE LAHU:	Mammu! Walua. Do you know your man does this?
WALUA:	Quintal, is a good man. He has given me children.
FASTO:	These things would not happen on Tahiti!
WALUA:	*(To MATA.)* You should cover your tits up.
TE LAHU:	No Tahitian will ever find happiness on Pitcairn.
WALUA:	English women wrap up their tits.
FASTO:	I want to go back to Tahiti.
TE'O:	I don't.
WALUA:	Me and Te'o, we're happy here. We have English husbands.
TE'O:	Land.
WALUA:	Children.
TE LAHU:	We can return to Tahiti.
FASTO:	We have no ship.
TE'O:	Even if you had a boat, you don't know where Tahiti is.
TE LAHU:	Titreano has The Bounty star reader. He can find Tahiti. But I saw him standing on the cliff yesterday. Where Paurai jump.
TE'O:	Pushed.
TE LAHU:	I hid, said nothing, he looked down at the stones below.
TE'O:	Ned Young is pumping his wife.
WALUA:	That baby of hers will be black.

FASTO: He loved Mi Mitti too much.

TE'O: Mi Mitti is nothing special.

WALUA: She walks about Pitcairn like a queen.

FASTO: She is a queen.

WALUA: I know.

FASTO: What do you mean then?

WALUA: What I mean is, who does she think she is?

FASTO: She thinks she's a queen.

WALUA: I know.

TE'O: You're an idiot.

WALUA: You keep your tits covered up.

Te Lahu Does anyone know if Titreano is eating? Mata?

MATA: Why would I know?

TE'O: Because your husband is pumping his wife!

WALUA and TE'O laugh.

TE'O: Has Ned stopped sleeping with you?

MATA: Yes. He says I am manuhane and he is ra'atira.

WALUA: So who are you having sex with then?

TE'O: Stay away from McKoy or I'll kill you.

MATA: Te Lahu, do you think Titreano is suicidal?

WALUA: How long can a man go without a tumble?

TE LAHU: Titreano is our only chance of leaving Pitcairn. We need to protect him, like a child. From both himself, and from Ned Young and his friends.

FASTO: Te Lahu, you are arioi, I am scared, what will happen to us?

TE LAHU: Your man will kill your man, and your man will kill your man, and your man will kill my man.

MATA: What about Hiti?

WALUA: You like Hiti?

TE'O: You could have Titreano girl!

WALUA: How do we protect Titreano?

TE LAHU: We kidnap him.

NED and JOHN ADAMS approach. NED has his Bible.

MATA: Arrgh! Shit!!! Bible class!

TE LAHU stands.

TE LAHU: I am going to dance. You do their stupid book
               class, look stupid, like happy slaves, but inside
               be strong, we are taking control.

NED and ADAMS discuss that morning's class. TE LAHU slips away.

NED: They confound me John.

There is an artful fart amongst the women. They all giggle.

               See! Our Lord creating the world in seven days
               doesn't impress them half as much as an artful
               fart.

ADAMS: Give 'em the miracles like grapeshot. Who could
               not be swayed by Christ walking on water?

NED: Our women! They all surf. This morning I
               thought I'd try the demon possessed mute.

ADAMS: No! The *blind*, demon possessed mute.
               That's better.

NED: Why?

ADAMS: 'cause he's blind. As well as being demon
               possessed. It's more of a miracle then ain't it.

NED: A miracle is a miracle. Let's continue with the
               old testament. Solomon. At least they'll find the
               violence entertaining.

FASTO: Yourley tardey!

NED:	Yes, sorry. Good morning ladies. Today Mister Adams is going to talk about the wisdom of Solomon. John.
ADAMS:	Aye, King Solomon was really clever. He was the wisest man in Christendom.
NED:	It wasn't called Christendom at that time John.
ADAMS:	No? Why not?
NED:	Christ hadn't yet been born.
FASTO:	Woz Soloman good surfer samuz Christ?
NED:	Yes. He was the surfing champion of all Judea.
SOME WOMEN:	*(Very impressed.)* Ah!
ADAMS:	Solomon had seven hundred wives.
FASTO:	Him pump dem all?
NED:	Each of his wives got satisfaction by him, yes, once a week.
TE'O:	Na! Him pump one hundred times wuhn day?
ADAMS:	*(Looks to NED, gets a nod.)* Yes.
FASTO:	Him mus' him have balls semuz coconuts!
ADAMS:	Yes. He did.
NED:	And yet his wisdom was more remarkable than his –
TE'O:	– coconut balls?

They laugh.

NED:	Tell the ladies about his remarkable wisdom John.
ADAMS:	One day there was a dispute. Two women was claiming to be the mother of the one little babby.
FASTO:	Wa' not di true mother kill di thief woman?
ALL:	Eeyeuh! Yes!

59

ADAMS: Mammu! Solomon says 'I'll chop the babby in two and you can have half each'. See?

Beat. NED's head drops.

FASTO: Him stupid. Di bebe would die.

NED: He knew the real mother would protect her child, and save its life by giving it to the imposter. Which she subsequently did.

WALUA: So di true ma give di bebe te di thief woman?

SOME: No. / Aue! / Eeyeuh! *(General confused groaning.)*

FASTO: Dat be stupid as chopp di bebe up in pieces!

NED: Solomon had no intention of dividing the child.

WOMEN: *(Realisation.)* Ah! / Oh.

Enter TE LAHU. She performs a dance. MATA rings the bell.

WALUA: Eeyeuh!

FASTO: Arioi dance!!

MATA: Surprises!

All the men arrive except MENALEE. Enter MI MITTI, she is very pregnant. During the dance everyone gathers, drawn by the women cheering. TE LAHU charts MI MITTI's relationship with FLETCHER CHRISTIAN, illustrated by a white dildo, and then her seduction by NED, illustrated by a black dildo. TE LAHU mimes the nine month gestation of the child, and then gives birth to a black aubergine, which cries like a baby. The women scream their applause. A silence falls, and all look to CHRISTIAN.

CHRISTIAN: *(To MI MITTI.)* My wife. I thought you were resting. The child is imminent.

MI MITTI: I came to see the Arioi dance.

CHRISTIAN: And you women, what are you doing sitting around? Is there not cloth to be made?

FASTO: We am learn 'bout King Solomon.

CHRISTIAN: From John Adams and Ned Young? The first can barely read, and the second elects himself a prophet to the women.

NED: Why do you libel me?

CHRISTIAN: Your life is a libel on the commandments!

NED: Which one of the ten?

CHRISTIAN: Thou shalt not commit adultery!

ADAMS: That's not the first commandment.

CHRISTIAN: I don't have to start at the beginning you damned feculent inbred!

QUINTAL: Adultery ain't so bad, here, is it?

BROWN: I didn't think you were one for the book Mister Christian.

CHRISTIAN: We do not need a book to be civilised! I accuse Ned Young of adultery with my wife!

QUINTAL: A duel!

MCKOY: Swords or pistols?!

ADAMS: Ned Young would swear on the Bible and his innocence will be proven.

CHRISTIAN: That book means nothing to him. It is exclusively an alternative authority to me, to my yarning court, to what I could have built here. It allows him to reject my every innovation.

NED: Who twixt you and I talks most like a prophet? 'My every innovation'; 'alternative to me' 'my yarning court'. These are megalomaniac phrases worthy of Bedlam.

CHRISTIAN: I am not mad!

QUINTAL: Also heard in Bedlam!

CHRISTIAN: To be consumed by reasonable fury is not to be mad! This girl, who took my heart; upturned my world; transformed me from gentleman to rover; from officer to dead man; from sceptic to supplicant; for whom I took a ship, and cast my captain, my family, and my reputation to the sharks. This girl! With whom I fell into a fever of hope that transformed all the ill and pestilence of the world into dreams of a different future in Arcadia. This girl! I taught her English, she taught me Tahitian, I made her my wife, and I swore to worship her with my last breath. It seems this girl has betrayed me with this man, Ned Young, who, on the wooden world of the ship, I counted as a gentleman, an officer and a friend. But he, with only words, traduced me, diminished me, and then stole away the purpose of my days. I may not yet be mad, but I will never love again, and am condemned, by my proximity, as we all are approximate to each other on this fist of rock, to forty years of torment as witness to their cooing. I would rather spend my next forty years put to the rack. Mister McKoy build me a wheel!

MI MITTI: Titreano, you deceived me!

(To them all.) On Tahiti he told my father, the king –

QUINTAL: In English you damned bitch!

MI MITTI: – Him say he high born, but truth is him family has no land, no houses, no wealth.

QUINTAL: I said –

CHRISTIAN: Let her have her say.

MI MITTI: Him lie to me, and him lie to you the night he sailed from Tahiti. It is I who has been betrayed, insulted, and disrespected.

MCKOY: What d'yer say to them? Yer speak English! Come on!

MI MITTI: Him family not ra'atira, them manuhane!

Grumblings amongst the Tahitians.

CHRISTIAN: Why in this land of plenty, where we could all have too much, are you still fettered by prejudice? God made no social divisions. 'When Adam delved and Eve span, where then was the gentleman?'

ADAMS: You ain't a believer, so don't go enlisting God's wisdom.

CHRISTIAN: Those words were written by a man.

ADAMS: Who?

BROWN: The preacher John Ball. Leader of the Peasants' revolt.

CHRISTIAN: We are born equal, the only divisions are of our own invention! Ha!

ADAMS: What's funny?

CHRISTIAN: But it should come to this! We had this island! This virgin leaf of velum! So perfect a sanctuary, and what have we done with it? We have stained it, soiled it with our traditions both English, and Tahitian.

TE LAHU: Youwuz talk talk fe dis man samuz dis man an' dis man samuz dis man. Wot bout de woman?

CHRISTIAN: Women?

TE LAHU: Ah wuken too. Yowuz plenty ground, yowuz plenty goat, me none.

QUINTAL: You're a woman!

TE LAHU: Ay ken dat cock brain!

QUINTAL advances but is held back by MCKOY.

CHRISTIAN: Your husband, Mister Brown, has an equal share of the island. So you are equal.

TE LAHU: Wosing me ground?!

CHRISTIAN: Your husband's land is your land.

QUINTAL pushes TE LAHU back.

BROWN: Can we return to the matter in hand and not be distracted by the fantastical. Ned Young. You stand accused of a serious crime.

NED: I am innocent of these charges.

CHRISTIAN: Thou shalt not bear false witness!

BROWN: Ned, would you swear on the book?

NED: Without hesitation.

BROWN takes the Bible from ADAMS. He steps forward, and holds it before NED.

BROWN: Place your hand on the book.

NED does so.

Er… Let me think how to word this.

CHRISTIAN: Have you lain with my wife?! Have you soiled this woman with your foul seed?!

BROWN: Thank you. Er…what he said.

NED: No. I have not.

CHRISTIAN: Ha! On the Bible!!
(Mainly to ADAMS.) And when that whore's child is born black you will take a minute to consider this day.

CHRISTIAN turns and exits to his cave.

QUINTAL: The sport's over lads. Back to work!

The men disperse. BROWN collars a somewhat reluctant WILLIAMS and they follow CHRISTIAN up to the eyrie, this is seen by NED. The women disperse. HITI throws a banana at MATA.

MATA: Why are you throwing fruit at me little boy?

HITI: Do you want to go fishing? With me.

MATA: No. Why would I?

HITI:	To get some fish.
MATA:	*(Laughing.)*
HITI:	It's fun. We can swim. I know a pool that gets hot.
MATA:	I haven't eaten yet.
HITI:	No, don't eat. You shouldn't eat and then go swimming, you might drown.
MATA:	That's why I said no, to fishing, with you.
HITI:	I know you love me. You brought me water when I was chained. You don't have a husband now.
MATA:	You're a boy.
HITI:	Me heart feels full for you.
MATA:	You're boiling over are you?
HITI:	Yes I am. I'll catch a whole basket of fish for you. Mata, I promise.
MATA:	Where is this hot pool?
HITI:	Near Paurai drop off.
MATA:	Let's go then big man.
HITI:	Aye, aye.

She walks off, he's shocked, but turns to the audience and gives a double thumbs up, and runs off.

End of scene.

ACT 3
SCENE 2

CHRISTIAN in his eyrie with BROWN.

CHRISTIAN: Have you come to offer me your wife?

BROWN: No, my loyalty, and an idea.

CHRISTIAN: The yarning court is the mortar and the men the pestle to crush all ideas.

BROWN: You know that Quintal raped Fasto?
And yesterday he lashed Menalee and rubbed salt in his wounds.

CHRISTIAN: For sport?

BROWN: What other reason could there be.

CHRISTIAN: Then it is excused, for it is sport we lack!

BROWN: We should kill Quintal. And McKoy.

CHRISTIAN: This is your idea? A man of your intelligence.

BROWN: Think of it like we're a crop and we have a blight. You'd cut it out.

CHRISTIAN: Do you propose a fair trial? Or something more summary.

BROWN: We kill them in their sleep. You are my captain. My only hope. I fear for my own skin. Quintal and McKoy are not the sum of our troubles. Menalee has a musket, hidden away. He intends to kill us all, the English men.

CHRISTIAN: How do you know this?

BROWN: Mareva, Menalee's wife, told Fasto. He might spare Ned Young. Because he is taio to him. And Ned and Adams are close because of their faith so that is three men. And we are three.

CHRISTIAN: Two surely.

BROWN: Three. Hiti, your taio, would be faithful.

CHRISTIAN: Yes, he would. Why do wish to align with me?

BROWN: I have no desire to live under the cosh of the Bible.

CHRISTIAN: This hill is defendable. The cave a redoubt.

BROWN: We should supply it. Meat, water, powder.

CHRISTIAN: We could start at first light. Give me your hand.

BROWN proffers his hand, but it turns into hug with CHRISTIAN sobbing.

End of scene.

ACT 3
SCENE 3

MI MITTI, heavily pregnant, and NED at MI MITTI's house. Dark.

NED: I have offered Menalee my wife, and Brown's gardens if he kills Brown. We can populate this island how we wish, and deliver the paradise of our imaginations. As queen, who would you be without?

MI MITTI: I keep all women.

NED: For contrast. None matches your beauty.

MI MITTI: I can no be Queen alone.

They kiss, and move into an embrace.

Go through the roll. I can no live with Quintal.

NED: I know how to reduce Quintal. What of McKoy?

MI MITTI: McKoy is a pig. Drink at sunrise, drink all day, drink at sunset. What kind of fool is this?

NED: He's Scottish. But even drunk he's a fine white iron man.

MI MITTI: Them anchors, them all nails now. What we need him for?

NED: He mends the hoes.

MI MITTI: And threatens owuz lives.

NED catches his breath, sits suddenly, holds his chest.

Wosing dat? You siki?

NED: Nothing. I've not eaten today.

NED: William Brown?

MI MITTI: His face disgusts me. That scar.

NED: Scrophula. We call it the King's Evil. Brown is invaluable, as a horticulturalist.

MI MITTI: Owuz gardens are all grow grow. I can no look at him.

67

NED:	The boy Hiti? We must have some men to work the land.
MI MITTI:	Hiti is taoi to Titreano. Him must take revenge. You has Menalee as a slave.
NED:	And Adams. Now, all rests on the timing. Shakespeare's tragedies take an age, and audience and hero succumb to the delays. Racine would have this done in a day, and that day must be tomorrow. Tahitian women can induce an aborsement of a child, can you also bring forward parturition?
MI MITTI:	Titreano no teach me teach me word?
NED:	Birth. The birth of your child as a part of the plan needs to be tomorrow.
MI MITTI:	Eeyeuh! Owuz women make baby come when ready, and ready now.
NED:	Tomorrow then, at first light. All the women would attend your labours, and would thus neither be able to defend their husbands. The sound of your pains, if artfully increased, might hide, or explain the other work. Tomorrow.

NED turns to go but faint and dizzy, steadies himself.

MI MITTI:	Again. You siki? You have him gripe?
NED:	No. It's nothing. I'll eat at my house.
MI MITTI:	Don't leave me alone.
NED:	I need to alert John Adams, to God's work, and his part in it. I will spend the night with you.

End of scene.

ACT 3
SCENE 4

CHRISTIAN's cave, night. BROWN, CHRISTIAN and HITI. BROWN is priming muskets. Provisioning, building defences.

CHRISTIAN's eyrie. CHRISTIAN and HITI.

CHRISTIAN: The opposite of taoi is enemy.

HITI: Owuz no word.

CHRISTIAN: We English do.

HITI: Wosing?

CHRISTIAN: Enemy.

HITI: Enimi.

CHRISTIAN: Ned Young is my enemy. And Menalee is his taio. My enemy's taio must be my enemy.

HITI: Eeyeuh!

CHRISTIAN: And yet you sleep at Menalee's house.

BROWN: That must end. Now.

HITI: Eeyeuh!

CHRISTIAN: Sleep in the woods tonight. Do you like Mata?

HITI: Mata? Mataohu. Mmmm. Her es goodahn!

CHRISTIAN: She will be your wife. Your tiro.

HITI: Mi tiro!? Mataohu! Wo dis?

CHRISTIAN: There will be a war. You, me, and Mister Brown, we fight together.

HITI: What day dis war begin?

CHRISTIAN: When we choose.

BROWN: Take this. It is primed.

BROWN gives him a musket.

HITI: Yoo wan me kill him Ned Young?

CHRISTIAN: Kill my enemy, yes. Ned Young, John Adams, and Menalee.

HITI: Disday?

CHRISTIAN: Tomorrow. Wait in the woods. Listen for musket fire and then advance upon them from behind their lines. There will be glory, and for you –

HITI: – Mata?

CHRISTIAN: Yes.

HITI runs off.

CHRISTIAN: Not yet two years in the Garden of Eden and we have a civil war.

BROWN: We will benefit doubly from their deaths. Two women would become available. Or do you wish to spend the rest of your life a widower, living in a cave, staring out to sea, seeing Bligh in every cloud.

CHRISTIAN: At night I have the stars, and yes, Bligh's imminent return is enough to fill the day.

BROWN: Bligh is dead sir.

CHRISTIAN: No, no, no! He lives! No finer navigator has ever been born. He's on the ocean now, headed this way, with a following wind. He comes to hang me! *(Beat.)* Don't look at me like that! I am not mad. That is reason. I know the man and I have done my calculations.

BROWN: Running down mutineers is not a job for Bligh. It's a task for a post captain, a man o' war and fifty marines.

CHRISTIAN: Yes, you're right.

BROWN: Bligh and Banks'll be back out after the bread fruit.

CHRISTIAN: Thank you. A sobering thought.

BROWN: In the morning, I'll harvest some yams, and plantains. Then we'll be provisioned.

End of scene.

ACT 3
SCENE 6

Dark. HITI asleep in a tree. He has a musket with him. Enter MATA.

MATA: Hiti!

HITI: Wa dat?! Ay ha' musket. Ay no freud te use him!

MATA: It's me. Mata!

HITI: What are you doing out here in the woods?

MATA: I could ask the same of you.

HITI: There will be a war tomorrow. And I am hiding.

MATA: I found you.

HITI: Yes, how did you find me here? This my secret
               place.

MATA: The pool where we bathe every morning is just
               there, and every morning you hide in this iron
               wood tree and watch us.

HITI: You know about me hiding in the tree watching
               you bathe?

MATA: Yes.

HITI: Oh no.

MATA: I knew you would be here.

HITI: So you came looking for a kiss then?

MATA: I'm scared. Mister Ned has spent all night
               priming muskets, and he told me that tomorrow
               I must be tiro to Menalee.

HITI: Ned Young has given you to Menalee as tiro?

MATA: I would rather die than have that fat bull on top
               of me every night.

HITI: I want to be your tiro.

MATA: You're a bit young for me

HITI: I make you laugh. And there's no one else.

71

MATA: Titreano has no wife.

HITI: You must want Titreano more than me.

MATA: No. He's sad. Crazy.

HITI: He is my taio, you mustn't speak like that of
           him, but yes, I agree, he is too crazy to be your
           husband. You need a young, funny, normal man
           like me.

MATA: Can I sit with you?

HITI: Yes, climb up.

She does.

MATA: Hold me. I'm scared.

HITI snatches a kiss.

           Don't be so quick. We've got all night.

They kiss. The night sets in dark.

ACT 4
SCENE 1

*Lights up. Sunrise. NED is standing outside MCKOY's house. He is
suffering from a mild tachypnea – rapid breathing. Not a cough, but
the rapid breathing breaks up his speech. QUINTAL's house is next door.*

NED: Mister McKoy! *(Breaths.)* It's me, Ned Young! Is
           anyone home! McKoy, it's me, Ned Young!

Enter HITI, swaggering in like a man.

HITI: *(Direct address.)* Surfing is for little boys. I can
           smell her on me. Strange. The smell, that was a
           surprise. I thought it would be sweet, but it's not,
           it's like a plant you find, deep in the roots of a
           tree. Rub the leaf, stain your fingers. Wash and it
           is still there. I like it. Do you remember that
           good days are…life, bad days are…history.
           The next history day, the next bad day, is today,
           dawning bright, and beautiful, the first day of my
           life as a man.

WALUA comes out.

NED: *(Surprised.)* Mrs Quintal?

WALUA: Wut a way you?

NED: I thought this was McKoy's house.

MCKOY comes out, and fondles WALUA.

MCKOY: It is.

NED: Have you exchanged wives?

Enter QUINTAL.

MCKOY: I was gyte with the horn last nite but mine
            wouldn't let me tup her so Quintal had tae
            lend me his.

NED: How utilitarian.

QUINTAL: You're grinding Christian's girl so go wipe your
            arse.

MCKOY: Aye, at least what we does is above board.

QUINTAL: You're out of breath fellah. Hey girl, get him
            some water.

WALUA goes off and gets water.

MCKOY: It's nae that hot man.

NED: It's a fever, I get, the only inheritance I will ever see.

Enter TE'O bandaged across the head, she is whimpering.

NED: Mrs McKoy, you're injured?

TE'O: Him bit dis wun ear off.

MCKOY: Aye, she wouldnae let me, so I skelped her one –

NED: And bit her ear off?

MCKOY: Dinna fash yersel with her singing.

WALUA returns with water.

QUINTAL: Sit yourself man, and slake your throat with that.

NED:	Brown told me that you are having no success distilling from sugar beet.
QUINTAL:	What's it to you?
NED:	I've been drinking rum longer than either of you. My wet nurse on St. Kitts gave me a thimble every night.
MCKOY:	We have nae yeast.
NED:	I can help, in exchange for a supply.

QUINTAL and MCKOY exchange glances, nods.

MCKOY:	Aye, that's braw.
NED:	Mister Brown tells me the root of the ti tree has yeast.
QUINTAL:	The ti tree?
NED:	The root. There's an abundance of ti trees on the western side, near the waterfall.

MCKOY starts to gather up the still etc.

MCKOY:	That's my day decided then.
NED:	I'd join you. But I'm on a hog shoot with Adams.
MCKOY:	Yee nae fit to hunt man.
NED:	Needs must. If you hear musket fire, that's us, not Bligh and a company of marines.
QUINTAL:	*(To MCKOY.)* Are we sleeping out?
MCKOY:	Aye, man, I'm not hauling that machine there and back for no purpose. And we got tae find the roots, and boil up a mash. That's more than a day.
QUINTAL:	Oi! Te'o, wrap us some meat up will you, yer sweet little skate!?

TE'O goes in.

| NED: | I'll come out and find you tomorrow. Equipped with a cup. |

NED walks off.

End of scene.

ACT 4
SCENE 2

TE LAHU, TE'O and FASTO, climb the path to CHRISTIAN's eyrie. CHRISTIAN is armed.

CHRISTIAN: Stay! Show your arms!

TE LAHU: Owuz women come fe get you come see di bebe.

CHRISTIAN: She's had the child?

FASTO: Eeyeuh!

CHRISTIAN: I heard nothing. No cries of labour.

TE LAHU: *(Beat.)* Mi Mitti woz baby mother afore.

CHRISTIAN: It may be easier second time, but not that easy.

TE'O: Him little little boy.

CHRISTIAN: A boy?

TE LAHU: Es him white boy.

ALL: Eyeugh!

FASTO: Mi Mitti...she wan talk fe you.

TE'O: Her heart big fe you.

FASTO: Yoo gwen come see dis bebe.

CHRISTIAN: Where is Ned Young?

FASTO: Him feelun siki siki disday. Fiva has him in his grip.

TE'O: Him na wan see di baby.

FASTO: He ken di baby white.

CHRISTIAN lowers his muskets and walks towards them, through them, and on down the slope. TE LAHU pushes FASTO up into the cave, whispers something in her ear. TE LAHU follows the party down.

End of scene.

ACT 4
SCENE 3

At NED's house. ADAMS and NED. NED's health is now moving towards an Acute Chest Syndrome Crisis caused by his Sickle Cell Anaemia. The symptoms of this are tachynpea (rapid breathing) and dyspnea (breathlessness). He does not have a cough, but does have chest pains, of a pulmonory nature, not heart.

NED: Did you sleep well last night John?

ADAMS: Grand. Aye. I had me supper, and a tot of rum, said me prayers, then I give her one, and that were enough to send me off.

NED: I'll put it in the log.

ADAMS: Ha! I'd rather you didn't!

Rapid breathing from NED. He hangs on to the table.

      Sailed with a darkie had this off Malagasy.

NED: I pray he lived?

ADAMS: For a day.

NED: I hope you gave him a Christian burial?

ADAMS: We chucked him overboard.

NED: Did you see Mister Brown.

ADAMS: Aye, he's in his gardens. He give me a wave.

NED: Which tells us what John?

ADAMS: That he ain't in the right mood for a Christian massacre.

NED: So their attack might come tomorrow? But we can better defend ourselves by using time to our advantage.

ADAMS: Attack before they are prepared?

NED: As General Wolfe surprised the French at Quebec. Prime this John.

Enter MENALEE.

MENALEE:	Yo rah nah! Me taoi!
NED:	Maita'i. Brown is in his gardens. Engage him in conversation. When you have his confidence, use the hatchet.
MENALEE:	You sikie sikie?
NED:	*(Angry.)* Never mind me! Avoid the musket, excepting necessity.
ADAMS:	Bring us his head.
NED:	Do you understand?
MENALEE:	I ken good. Kill him Brown. Wa bout Titreano?
NED:	Mister Christian is in his cave. Which he can defend.
MENALEE:	Mi feart fe Mister Quintal. Ay freten.
NED:	Quintal and McKoy will be west and over the ridge. Consumed.
MENALEE:	Wosing Mata. Me tiro! You kah say wosing place she be?
NED:	She's on Pitcairn. Somewhere. And she's yours. Now go.
MENALEE:	Aye, aye.

MENALEE leaves. NED is breathing rapidly, and is in full tachypnea crisis.

ADAMS:	Can God see us now? Indoors?
NED:	He can see indoors.
ADAMS:	And we're not doing wrong in his eyes?
NED:	The Bible says that those who live by the false prophets of drink and licentiousness shall meet with swift destruction.
ADAMS:	Which gospel is that?
NED:	One of the early ones.

End of scene.

ACT 4
SCENE 4

A still is set up with the copper coil running through a waterfall. QUINTAL and MCKOY are both intent on watching the distillation. One drip comes through.

MCKOY: There's a jill.

QUINTAL: Jill my arse, it's like a Persian faucet!

MCKOY takes the cup from the still. QUINTAL snatches if from him.

Give it here yer damned arseworm!

QUINTAL sniffs it, pulls a face, not at the smell but at its obvious strength.

No sea too rough, no muff too tough!

He swigs it down.

MCKOY: What's it taste of man?

QUINTAL: Jesus! It's terrible.

MCKOY: Can you drink it?

QUINTAL: We got no choice do we, you damned sheep biter!

QUINTAL snatches a drink of water. A distant musket shot is heard. They freeze in fear.

MCKOY: Bligh?

QUINTAL: Ned Young hunting pigs.

MCKOY has a cup now, he sniffs, doesn't like the smell.

Come on man!

MCKOY takes a gulp.

Here, you'll need water, or you'll lose your tongue.

MCKOY swigs some water.

MCKOY: Ach! It's just the damnedest thing that any man slung down his neck.

QUINTAL: Jesus!

QUINTAL holds his cock and staggers around.

MCKOY: What is it man?

QUINTAL: It's gone straight to me romantics. God man,
            you've made a potion for the venereals!

MCKOY takes a bite of fruit, a cucumber or something.

MCKOY: Christ! Do you need the fruit or nae!?

QUINTAL: I've ne'er felt like this. I could fuck a tree.

QUINTAL walks off holding his cock.

MCKOY: Where you going man!?

QUINTAL: I'm gonna find mesel a good looking tree.

End of scene.

ACT 4
SCENE 5

*Indoors at NED's place. ADAMS and NED. NED is kneeling on the floor,
breathing rapidly, holding his chest. Technically, medically, he is mid
Acute Chest Syndrome and is under pulmonary straina and also suffering
rapid heart – tachycardia. ADAMS stands over him.*

NED: I can't slow my heart!

ADAMS: You know this well then?

NED: On St Kitts. In the Africans.

ADAMS: I always said you're no quadroon. You got more
            than a touch of the tar brush then, you got their
            blighted blood an'all.

NED: Punch my chest, here. You will outlive me John,
            so listen good. The women are the real task.
            Do not let them imagine a world where women
            have advantage, for if they can imagine it today,
            they might have it tomorrow. And what would
            that mean for us John?

ADAMS: Dunno er…dunno.

NED: Slavery.

ADAMS kneels and punches NED's chest. Enter MENALEE bloodied, carrying the basket covered with a bloodied cloth.

MENALEE: Yoo siki siki! Water!

ADAMS: He's got water. It ain't no use.

MENALEE puts BROWN's head on the table.

MENALEE: Mister Brown! See!

ADAMS: You've blown his damned brains clean out the back of his head.

MENALEE: Ai. I like him good Mister Brown.

NED is on his knees, holding his chest, breathing rapidly.

NED: Get that head out of my sight!

MENALEE: In war owuz folk lash up dead man head on dem belt.

He ties the head by the hair on to his belt.

                Where be Mata? My tiro? She come here?

ADAMS: I ain't seen her.

MENALEE: Titreano come down fe top, come see Mi Mitti an' di bebe.

NED: She's had the child?

MENALEE: Mus do.

NED: Have you seen it?

MENALEE: No.

NED: In the cave Christian was safe, but not now. You know what to do?

MENALEE: Aye, aye. Ay kill him, bring yuz him head. Mata me tiro disday, aye aye!

NED: Yes, she is yours!

MENALEE exits. ADAMS sits at the table. NED chest pains, breathless.

ADAMS: That's a fair churchyard cough you got there sir.

NED: I'm dying John. Pitcairn will be yours. For God.

End of scene.

ACT 4
SCENE 6

Outside MI MITTI's house. The women enter with CHRISTIAN amongst them. TE LAHU trips CHRISTIAN.

MI MITTI: Kneel!

CHRISTIAN: Where is my wife?

They jump him and manacle him, he puts up a fight.

What is this?

TE LAHU: Yorley mek boat fe us, we sail big water.

FASTO: *(Wielding the sextant.)* Yorley come fe us, point one way, point anudderone way.

CHRISTIAN: I am no use to you without the star charts.

TE LAHU: We got all yus papers.

FASTO: We don't have to speak your stupid language any more.

CHRISTIAN: What did you say?

TE'O: Owuz women no kah speak arsewipe English no more disday!

TE LAHU: Youz stole stole us fe Tahiti. Fe mi children.

Enter MI MITTI.

CHRISTIAN: Where's my baby? It's black isn't it. Where's Ned Young?

MI MITTI: Him siki siki.

TE LAHU: Our Queen. Come speak to me.

They go out of earshot of CHRISTIAN.

Where is the baby?

81

MI MITTI: Dead.

TE LAHU: The baby died?

MI MITTI: Ned Young lied to me. He is sick, and he knew
                he was sick.

TE LAHU: These English lie, to get what they want.

MI MITTI: It is as if they they don't know that it is not
                possible to lie on an island. Perhaps England is
                so big that it is possible to lie, and not be found out.

TE LAHU: I hate them.

MI MITTI: My father was confused by their ships, their iron,
                their muskets. So he made them gods, and set
                them high above us, when there is nothing they
                have that we ever wanted or needed.

TE LAHU: Are you with us then now.

MI MITTI: It is my obligation to return to Tahiti and destroy
                everything English, every nail, every mirror,
                every piece of jewelry. No one will be allowed
                to even talk about the English and we will attack
                any ship that comes into the bay!

Enter HITI and MATA. HITI is armed with a musket.

HITI: What have you done with Titreano!?

TE'O: He is our prisoner.

HITI: No! He is my taio!

TE LAHU raises her musket at HITI.

TE LAHU: I will shoot.

HITI drops the musket. FASTO picks it up.

TE LAHU: We're running the island now. The Women.

TE'O: *(To MATA.)* Are you and Hiti tiro now then?

SOME   Oooh! / ha, ha. /

WALUA: Where did you do it?

TE'O: In his tree!?

Laughter.

FASTO: Why is Hiti sitting here? He's not a woman.

TE'O: Aye, piss off. Sit over there with your taio.

HITI moves to near CHRISTIAN.

TE LAHU: We must decide what to do with the other men.

FASTO: Kill them!

WALUA: Don't be stupid.

TE'O: Who would build the boat?

TE LAHU: If we all live here, in one house, we can kill
               the men, we can pull down the other houses
               and use the boards to build a boat.

WALUA: You're not pulling down my house!

TE LAHU: Mammu! Let us discuss the men first, one by one.

HITI moves and sits with CHRISTIAN.

TE LAHU: Shall we spare John Adams to help build the boat.

TE'O: I'm not going to sea in a boat built by an idiot.

TE LAHU: Mister Adams, your husband, do you want to
               speak for him?

WALUA: Is he an idiot?

FASTO: Yes.

TE'O:/WALUA: Kill him!

FASTO: If you kill him will I keep the gardens?

TE LAHU: That is all determined by how we decide to live.

FASTO: No! No one is taking my gardens from me!
               I married an Englishman.

TE'O: What happened in the past doesn't matter now.

TE LAHU: Do you want to work your gardens alone?

FASTO: Yes! They are my gardens.

TE LAHU: We can have one big garden and share the labour.

FASTO: I own the land from the aute forest to Brown's
            fence and when I die it is my children's.

WALUA: I thought you wanted to go back to Tahiti.

FASTO: I do but whilst the boat is being built, or if the
            boat sinks.

TE LAHU: The best man to build a boat would be McKoy.

FASTO: A drunk.

TE LAHU: A blacksmith. Te'o, he is your husband.

TE'O: I never want to see him again. He bit my ear off.

FASTO: And he is taoi to Quintal, who must die.

WALUA: Why do you want to kill my man?

FASTO: He raped me.
            Kill them both!

WALUA stands.

WALUA: No! He has given me children. I love him.

WALUA exits running.

TE'O: If we kill all the men, what do we do for sex?

MATA: We will have three men!

FASTO: Titreano, Adams and Hiti.

TE LAHU: Sex for them is a payment for good work on the
            boat.

TE'O: Hiti?

FASTO: Hiti is a man now!

ALL: Eeyeuh! / Ah yes! / That's clever. / Of course!

*MENALEE steps forward, musket raised. He has BROWN's head tied to
his belt by the hair. The women stand and wield their muskets.*

TE LAHU: Stop!

MENALEE: Mata! Girl. You're my tiro now. Ned Young has given you to me.

HITI: No! Mataohu is my tiro.

HITI steps between him and MATA. MENALEE fires on HITI who is hit, and falls dying. TE'O fires. MENALEE is hit, falls and drops his musket.

MENALEE: Te'o. You shot me?!

TE'O: I did. Mareva is your wife, not Mata.

MENALEE: My mana is gone.

MENALEE dies. MATA is left holding HITI who is dying.

MATA: Hiti! Hiti! Talk to me!

HITI: I can see you. Touch me.

MATA kisses his lips.

We were together, once. Only once, but once. Yes?

MATA: Yes. It was beautiful.

HITI: My mana is gone now.

MATA: No! Hiti! Don't close your eyes. Hiti!

He dies.

TE LAHU: His mana has gone to the gods.

ALL: *(As a respectful chant.)*
Let his mana play with the gods
Let his mana kiss the gods
Let his mana be a god

FASTO: His mana has gone.

Enter JOHN ADAMS unarmed. TE LAHU points a musket at him.

TE'O: Yoo kah pahs!

ADAMS: I heard the shots. I want my wife. Fasto. *(To FASTO.)* Go home girl.

TE LAHU:	Yoo no tumble her disday!
ADAMS:	I'll tumble my wife whenever I likes and I don't have to beg your approval. What is this?
TE LAHU:	All Pitcairn groun es ours disday.
ADAMS:	By what right?
TE LAHU:	Fe musket.
MATA:	Owuz women got all muskets.
ADAMS:	No you aint, I got one back at my house.
TE LAHU:	Te'o! Quick! Go and get Adams musket.
ADAMS:	Oh bugger!
TE'O:	No. I'm scared. I'm not going on my own. I don't know where Quintal is.
TE LAHU:	Sit yorley arse on ground!
TE'O:	Or yoo gwen fetch yorley balls in yon water?!

ADAMS sits.

ADAMS:	*(To CHRISTIAN.)* What are you doing?
CHRISTIAN:	I have to build them a boat. And you're to help me.
ADAMS:	Are you enslaved?
CHRISTIAN:	I am.

TE LAHU chucks a set of manacles at ADAMS on the ground.

TE LAHU:	Yorley put iron on foot now!
CHRISTIAN:	And so are you.
TE LAHU:	*(To ADAMS.)* Wosing your taio, Ned Young?
ADAMS:	Aye, he's badly. Breathing like a leaking bellows.
FASTO:	It's true, I seen him. He's lying on the mud outside his house.
TE'O:	What do we do?

TE LAHU: We need to control all the muskets. Then tomorrow we will hunt down Quintal and McKoy. Fasto, and Te'o get Adams musket and bring Ned Young here. Bind him, make him secure.

FASTO: We have no more manacles.

TE'O: We could nail him to a plank of wood.

MI MITTI: He would want to die like his god, on a cross.

TE'O: Yes, it would be really funny!

TE LAHU: No sentiments! No sympathy! These men enslaved us!

MATA: So why do you want to keep him alive?

TE LAHU: He can work the star machine.

TE'O: But we have Titreano for that.

TE LAHU: If Quintal kills Titreano, and we have killed Ned Young, then we are lost.

TE'O and FASTO exit. HITI stands and walks to the front of stage for direct address.

HITI: Now it is unusual for the narrator to be killed in the middle of his own story?! But that is Pitcairn. Everything is different on Pitcairn. There are no rules. But at least I did not die a boy. I knew love, and died a man. But I do not know what happens next so I will sit and watch the next history day with you.

HITI sits in the audience.

End of scene.

ACT 4
SCENE 7

MCKOY by the waterfall. Asleep, dead drunk. Enter WALUA, with a child at her breast.

WALUA: *(Shouting loud.)* Matty! Ay got wickles!

She kicks MCKOY awake.

           Bill McKoy! Wa sing yourley doin!? Wosing be my man Quintal?

MCKOY: Arghh! Strewth!

WALUA: Ay bring yoo pork an' egg.

MCKOY wakes.

MCKOY: Yous a fine braw lassie, Walua. Come here yer bonny wee bundle.

MCKOY makes a grab at her, she fights him off.

WALUA: Gwen wipe! Ay no wan no bedtime working. Ay got di bebe on di tit.

MCKOY sits up.

MCKOY: Agh! Jesus! My damned heed!

WALUA finds a cup of rum.

WALUA: Yoo mekking rum eh?

MCKOY: Aye. It's damned powerful. Here.

He offers her some. He drinks it instead.

WALUA: Ay no wan rum disday. Us women come fe kill yoo disday. Us women ha' all musket. Wa bin my man?!

MCKOY: *(Shouting.)* Quintal! *(Holding his head.)* Jesus. What of Christian?

WALUA: Titreano him live on.

MCKOY: You got sweet wee dugs Walua.

MCKOY fondles her breasts. WALUA whacks him really hard.

WALUA: Kah foo yoo cock like wood so early disday?

MCKOY: The brew. It fires yer Venus.

WALUA: Eeyeugh!?

MCKOY: Aye, it makes your ready for loving.

WALUA: Gimme.

MCKOY gives her a drink.

              Agh!

MCKOY: Here, a wee shot of fruit calms it!

She snatches a bite, swallows.

WALUA: Ay like it damn good. Es hot! Unuderwun gimme!

MCKOY holds it back.

MCKOY: If you let me have a wee feel.

WALUA: Yoo be quick?

MCKOY: Aye.

MCKOY starts to grope her, she puts the baby aside, and climbs on top of her. Enter the women from both sides holding muskets and axes/knives. MATA is not with them. MCKOY grabs WALUA as a shield.

TE'O: Us cum fe to kill yoo disday.

MCKOY: Te'o?! You're my damned wife!

TE'O: If ay be yoo wife, who dat den?

Enter QUINTAL. MCKOY turns sees him. WALUA frees herself.

QUINTAL: You damned black bitches!

WALUA: Matty! Dey gwen kill yoo disday!

FASTO fires, misses.

QUINTAL: Aye, there's a knack to them old navy canons.

QUINTAL runs off.

TE LAHU: Let him go.

The women turn again to MCKOY. He drops to his knees. MCKOY is surrounded. The women close the circle. No one seems to want to make the first move. MCKOY assesses the situation, and reaches for the bottle.

MCKOY: A last dram!?

TE LAHU: Kah.

(TE LAHU kicks the cup over. MCKOY is tragic, desperate for the drink.)

MCKOY: Argh! Yous a lang shanked black witch, yous!

The women start to close in. We don't see him killed.

End of scene.

ACT 4
SCENE 8

CHRISTIAN and ADAMS are guarded by MATA with musket. NED YOUNG's hands are nailed to a plank, a single plank, not a crucifix. He is on his knees. He lives yet. ADAMS is feeding him water. The breathlessness and chest pains continue.

NED: God bless you John.

ADAMS: I'd pull them there nails out but that bitch won't let me.

MATA: Nuff! Nuff! Yus fe working build boat now disday!

NED: I need shade, John, please.

ADAMS: Aye, but me chain lacks the length to –

MATA: – Last time! Last time!

CHRISTIAN: So you will die like Christ.

NED: It's the only blessing in all this hell.

CHRISTIAN: You don't know, you might rise on the third day.

NED: My soul shall be content with Heaven.

CHRISTIAN: Heaven might be full. And your 'sins to good works' ledger won't balance, not if your God's been watching.

ADAMS: God forgives.

CHRISTIAN: God does but I don't. What about the Holy Ghost? Does he forgive?

NED: Why do you torture me with this rhetoric!

CHRISTIAN: I always think of him as a cantankerous old bugger.

NED: He is God, part of the trinity.

CHRISTIAN: God the Father, God the Son, and God the Holy Ghost. You'd think there would only be one God in a montheistic religion.

ADAMS: He's on his last breath man, don't give him `doubts now.

NED: I have no doubts John!

ADAMS: *(To MATA.)* He needs some shade, can I move him?

MATA: Speak Tahitian! You stupid cunt rag!

ADAMS: What did she say? You speak their tongue.

CHRISTIAN: She said – I like you Wreckless Jack, you're my favourite.

ADAMS: Aye? I seen her admirin' me. I could give her one. She's a ripe little doxy. If I weren't such a good Christian. And in chains. Ah forget it.

NED: Press my chest John. My chest!

ADAMS puts his foot on NED's chest.

NED: That helps, it helps.

CHRISTIAN: You have two toes missing. On your right foot.

ADAMS: Aye.

CHRISTIAN: What happened to them?

ADAMS: I got one in a pearl case back in Hackney,
            I dunno where the other is.

CHRISTIAN: I mean't, how did you lose them?

ADAMS: In that Bethnal Green Poor House of mine,
            one of them come at me with an axe. Aye, they
            was unreasonable fierce was our nuns.

CHRISTIAN: You deceived Bligh then, both in name and
            condition?

ADAMS: Bligh knows about the toes. He made me run the
            length of the dockside. It didn't slow me down,
            so he took me on.

CHRISTIAN: Will you be missed in England John Adams?

ADAMS: I'm an orphan, ain't I. London's glad to see the
            back of me. You, your mother'll be weeping
            before your portrait every day.

NED: He has no portrait. Help me John! Water!

TE LAHU and MI MITTI enter.

ADAMS: He's dying! You're his damn wife, you ripe little
            bitch!

TE LAHU: Don't talk to them.

CHRISTIAN: Taking orders now my darling?

TE LAHU: Speak Tahitian!

MI MITTI: Te Lahu has not lied to me. She is the spirit of
            Tahiti so I follow her.

*Enter the other women, except WALUA. TEO carries MCKOY's bloodied
head.*

MATA: Whose head is that?

TEO: McKoy, my husband.

TE LAHU: Quintal lives.

MATA: Why do you keep McKoy's head?

TEO: His land is mine, I have his head!

MATA: We agreed not to divide the land.

ADAMS: Someone's lost their head.

CHRISTIAN: McKoy. Te'o will use it as proof of her inheritance.

ADAMS: Aye, I seen that on Tahiti. Skulls on sticks outside the houses.

CHRISTIAN: The English have titles and deeds, and pay lawyers. They have their ancestors' skulls, and don't pay lawyers. We could discuss which is the better system.

ADAMS: Damn these chains!

CHRISTIAN: You don't like being enslaved by women then John?

ADAMS: If the Lord had wanted women to rule o'er men He woulda give 'em some particular advantage like, I dunno, longer arms.

CHRISTIAN: Longer arms?

ADAMS: Aye, or something equivalently useful.

CHRISTIAN: These women are like you Ned, they like their theatre! They're staging a passion! And you have the lead!

NED: I'd rather this than your fate. They'll drag you back to Deptford and string you from the yard arm and let you rot like a mole on a fence as a message to every tar in England.

ADAMS: They wouldn't hang me.

NED: They should hang you twice. Once for the mutiny and once for the levelling that led to this carnage.

CHRISTIAN: I have made mistakes. But I now know that the natural condition of man is violence, lechery, drunkeness, greed, suspician and hate. And there

> is a lesson learned – that man's free will needs
> an authority greater than that of a mere yarning
> court of mortal men. Maybe I do need God.

NED: Pitcairn! I die!

NED dies.

ADAMS: He's gone I think. He's right though. You ain't a
man of God.

CHRISTIAN: God does not need to exist in order to be useful
to me.

End of scene.

ACT 4
SCENE 9

*WALUA is on the cliff top with her child suckling at her breast. She puts
it down in the grass.*

WALUA: *(A scream. A second scream.)*
Mi Mitti has milk. You will not want for milk.
Your daddy gave me this on Tahiti years ago.
Look, it has never changed, it is as constant as
my love for him.

She ties the nail around the baby's neck.

> It is iron. A piece of England. You will grow to be
> like a nail, strong and rare, like an Englishman.

Baby cries.

> Don't cry, someone will come.

*Enter MATA, FASTO, TE'O all wielding muskets. WALUA starts backing
to the cliff.*

FASTO: Where's Quintal?

TE'O: Walua! What are you doing?!

WALUA: I have just fed the boy. Mi Mitti has milk.

TE'O: No! We are going home, in the boat, you will
          come with us.

FASTO: We're going back to Tahiti.

TE'O: Walua! Come away from the cliff!

WALUA: I was happy here.

WALUA throws herself off the cliff. MATA steps down stage for direct address.

MATA: We all know that good days are life, and
          get forgotten, and only bad days, history days,
          are remembered. That day, Menalee killed
          Brown, and the boy Hiti; Te'o killed Menalee;
          the women killed McKoy and Ned Young; and
          my friend Walua threw herself off the cliff. Ever
          since this rock of Pitcairn rose from the sea there
          has never been a more history day than this day.

HITI: Mata! Mata! I'm here!

MATA: For the next two months Fletcher Christian
          and John Adams, in chains, built the boat, and
          we women worked together fishing and farming,
          looking after the children. It sounds idyllic, but
          the mad dog Quintal was still at large. Imagine
          that. I want you to try and imagine that. Living
          on a small island, one English mile by two miles,
          with a mad dog on the loose.

HITI: Mata! I'm here!?

MATA: Sometimes in the night I thought I heard Hiti
          calling me.

HITI: Yes!

MATA: And I lay awake imagining a life with him.

HITI: Yes! Oh Mata'oha!

MATA: But it scared me. Pitcairn will not make me mad.
          The next history day is the day we launch the boat.

End of scene.

ACT 5
SCENE 1

The boat is built. A bright sunny day. CHRISTIAN and ADAMS, guarded by FASTO, and MI MITTI whose attention is divided between guarding them and pushing the baby in the crib. FASTO is asleep. CHRISTIAN looks to the heavens.

CHRISTIAN: What are we now? Two hours before midday?

ADAMS: What does time matter?

CHRISTIAN: Time is everything. The work's done, I'll get on with the caulking. What do you think? Will she float or will she founder?

CHRISTIAN: She'll founder.

ADAMS: No! With the hull caulked she'll be a fair little jolly boat. But we must caulk her good. Ten coats, ten more days. Why spoil the boat for a ha'peth of tar.

CHRISTIAN: No. We sail today, it has to be today.

ADAMS: Are you mad? It's not caulked, she'll sink.

CHRISTIAN: Don't give me away, or death's your portion.

ADAMS: Oh, I get it, you want the boat to sink. You got a scheme eh?

MI MITTI takes FASTO's pistol and approaches CHRISTIAN with it, at the same time as holding the baby. ADAMS sees her advance.

ADAMS: Mister Christian. Your wife's got herself a musket. And is aiming it at your head.

CHRISTIAN turns around.

CHRISTIAN: You would kill me?

MI MITTI: I want. I want.

CHRISTIAN: You can't. That would not serve your people. I can use the sextant. Kill me when we get to Tahiti. The musket is threatening, but that picanninny is the real violence.

MI MITTI shows the baby more deliberately.

MI MITTI: Ned loved me good. Like a man. You love me like a boy.

CHRISTIAN: Hurt on hurt. Pile it on. I have no feelings left.

MI MITTI: Ned kiss me good. Sweet.

CHRISTIAN: That's his profession. He's a coster monger of kissing.

MI MITTI: Ned love me long. Yowuz quick quick.

CHRISTIAN: You can't make me feel. I'm numb.

MI MITTI: I wash you away. Completely.

CHRISTIAN: Where's Thursday, our son? Who's looking after him?

MI MITTI: He is dead to me.

CHRISTIAN: He's too young to run wild. Will you take him in the boat?

MI MITTI: He is a dog now. Dogs run wild.

CHRISTIAN: What will your father do, to me, when I get you home.

MI MITTI: He will kill you with a knife.

CHRISTIAN: I didn't lie to him when I said that I am ra'atira. I am.

MI MITTI: You no ground in England.

CHRISTIAN: No land, no. But my blood is aristocratic, ra'atira. But I have nothing and that is not uncommon. The gambling debts of second sons ruin many a noble family, but it doesn't make them any the less noble.

MI MITTI: This I don't understand, how –

CHRISTIAN: – yes! This is our real failure, to dove tail our cultures, to understand, to sympathise instead of allow incredulity to wash away our love.

MI MITTI: Work. No talking.

CHRISTIAN: Give me your chisel.

CHRISTIAN takes ADAM's chisel. MI MITTI raises the musket. CHRISTIAN places it on his little toe of the right foot. With an intake of breath and a swift blow from the malet he chops off his toe.

CHRISTIAN: Aaargh!

Swiftly he does the same to the next toe.

ADAMS: What are you doing man?!

CHRISTIAN: Aargh!

The girls come forward.

ADAMS: You cut your toes off!

FASTO starts to care for him, with water, and dressings.

ADAMS: You lost your damned senses man!

QUINTAL appears out of the woods. He is wearing nothing but a loin cloth. He carries a bottle in one hand, a knife in the other. He grabs MI MITTI from behind. She screams. Loudly. He uses her as a shield during the next, wielding a knife.

ADAMS: Have you been drinking?

QUINTAL: I promised meself I'd dock this doxie afore
             I die. Got yer manacled eh Reckless Jack? Sick
             of your sermonising?

QUINTAL stabs him.

QUINTAL: – that'll shut you up your damned soul driver.

ADAMS is dead.

             (To CHRISTIAN.) In all your puff did ye ever meet
             a more complete idiot?

CHRISTIAN: Never. Is that alcohol? I could use some.

QUINTAL: You don't want to drink this, it'll make you hard,
             and if they don't give you a woman you'll go
             mad. But you're mad already.

QUINTAL throws him a bottle. He then forces a kiss on MI MITTI, she screams, so he thrusting a rag in her mouth. CHRISTIAN pours the alcohol on his wounded foot. It stings. He wails.

QUINTAL: What the hell you done with your foot man?

CHRISTIAN: An accident. With a chisel.

QUINTAL: Them's the self same toes that Wreckless Jack
             had missing. I know you, you're scheming.

QUINTAL mounts MI MITTI, penetrates. CHRISTIAN watches.

QUINTAL: Argh, yes. What are they keeping you for then?

CHRISTIAN: Navigation. Back to Tahiti.

QUINTAL: Clever. Giss it here! Giss it!

CHRISTIAN gives him the bottle and he swigs away as he thrusts. Enter TE LAHU with musket and encircles QUINTAL at a distance.

             Don't fire! Eh! I gots your queen under here.

TE LAHU: No musket fire!

QUINTAL: Let me finish. A tumble ain't a tumble without a
             finish. Is it? Then you can do your worst.

Suddenly TE'O dives in and whacks him on the head with the musket. Then all the women pile in. It is a frenzied, seemingly endless attack during which we can see QUINTAL use all his strength to fight the women off, at one point standing with three women clinging to him beating him down. The frenzy continues until he seems dead, knives sticking out of his back. The women step away. Suddenly he rises to his knees.

             Aargh! You damned black bitches! I'll see you
             in hell Fletcher Christian. After Pitcairn, it'll be
             a dove.

He dies.

TE'O: His mana is gone.

CHRISTIAN: We should give these men a Christian burial
             and offer their souls to God.

TE LAHU: God es storley, storley, storley. Es no white man
             god.

CHRISTIAN: It is true that at one time, blinded by conceit, invincible, lord of all I surveyed, I could not see Him, obscured as He was by mine own brilliance. But he has shown himself to me. He sent the Angel Gabriel to comfort me last night.

TE LAHU: You loy!

TE'O: Wot wickles you cook up for him?

CHRISTIAN: He'd already eaten. He told me that God did not make Eve to rule over Adam.

TE LAHU: Es storley!

CHRISTIAN: Here in his first creation, the garden of Eden. Yes, this island, Pitcairn, was the first garden. That's what Gabriel told me.

TE LAHU: Yorley loy loy loy.

CHRISTIAN: I am not lying. The Angel Gabriel told me that God is going to sink the boat. If we try to leave, and He will turn the day into night. He will place a great stone over the sun.

TE LAHU: We sail disday, now, disday! Is di boat complete.

CHRISTIAN: The work is finished.

MATA: Es done, es good disday.

TE LAHU: Load the boat. Put all those provisions in. And the fishing lines. The sextant, the charts. We must make the most of the light. Come on!

TE'O: We are scared!

MATA: Titreano is saying that their god will sink the boat.

TE'O: Their god will take the sun away and every day will be dark.

FASTO: Go wipe! The boat is finished, we can leave today.

TE'O: All their God stories are shit!

MATA: What about their god's son rising from the dead.

TE'O: I rise from the dead every morning.

MI MITTI: Titreano himself does not follow the English
           God. Many times he told me of his certainty that
           the Bible was a story written by men to control
           other men.

TE LAHU: – Mammu! That is an end to this talk! We have a
           task. We are going home. Let us carry the boat
           to the water.

*The women lift the boat. It starts to get dark as the moon begins to pass
across the sun.*

TE'O: It's getting dark!

MATA: It is the middle of the day.

FASTO: It is like Titreano said. Their God has placed his
           hand over the sun!

*Bedlam, screaming and prostrating towards the sun. CHRISTIAN watches.
And drops to his knees and begins to pray. During his prayer he encourages
the women to join him, and stop their wailing and running around.*

CHRISTIAN: Let us pray! Everone! Pray with me!

           O Lord our heavenly Father almighty
           and everlasting God, who safely brought
           us to this Eden accept now our unfeigned prayer

           (To TE LAHU.) Kneel!

           We now supplicate ourselves to thy Glorious Majesty,
           offer Thee our thanksgivings and beg for Thy
           Gracious Protection.

           We most devoutly thank thee for our
           preservation & are truly conscious that
           only through thy Divine intervention we have been
           saved from certain death at sea.

*CHRISTIAN has a crafty look up at the sun, to see how the eclipse is
progressing. It's in its third act so he too proceeds to the third act of the prayer.*

Everyone repeat this after me. Loudly, so He can hear! In English!
From this day forward

ALL: From disday.

CHRISTIAN: I promise to live my life.

ALL: Ay promise 'o live mi life.

CHRISTIAN: In accord with Thy Commandments

ALL: In cord wid di Command.

CHRISTIAN: As described by your instrument Titreano

ALL: As decribe by yoo instrument Titreano

CHRISTIAN: Who shall be known as Adam.

ALL: Who be ken by Adam.

CHRISTIAN: We, obey! Return us to the light!

ALL: We obey! Return us to di light!

The scene ends in the dark.

End of scene.

EPILOGUE

*Lights up on CAPTAIN PIPON and CAPTAIN STAINES sitting on a log.
STAINES is studying papers, books, the Bounty log.*

STAINES: I can't find a John Adams on the Bounty roll.

PIPON: Perhaps he didn't sign as an AB.

STAINES: I've been through the full complement, quarter deck and forecastle.

PIPON: Any Londoners?

STAINES: There's an Alexander Smith.

PIPON: Ah! Bligh describes an Alexander Smith.
Two toes missing from his right foot. 'To be spared. There was no room in the launch.'

Enter CHRISTIAN carried in a sedan chair by four women.

STAINES: We can't find you on the Bounty roll.

CHRISTIAN: I signed on as Alex Smith. My father, John
Adams were a thief, known to the navy, so for
Bligh I had myself invent a clean name,
Alexander Smith. A loyal man to Bligh I were.
I fetched him his breeches that morning to cover
his modesty. He'll have that writ down if I know
Bligh.

PIPON: No, he doesn't mention that.

STAINES: We'd like to inspect your right foot.

CHRISTIAN: Aye.

CHRISTIAN proffers his foot. One of the women take his boot off.

PIPON: What happened to your toes?

CHRISTIAN: I got one in a pearl case back in Hackney,
I dunno where the other is.

PIPON: Thank you.

CHRISTIAN: Has Bligh writ me down as a rebel?

STAINES: No. 'To be spared. No room in the launch.'

PIPON: Never in these islands have we seen such a
healthy, happy and devout colony. You have
claimed this island for the King and its people
for the Lord and you are its worthy governor.

CHRISTIAN: You don't want me 'ead then?

STAINES: You're a free man. Free to come with us, back to
England.

PIPON: Or free to stay. It is your choice.

CHRISTIAN: What would I return to? What's my reputation?

PIPON: John Adams is not known. England only knows
Christian.

CHRISTIAN: And what do they say of that unfortunate wretch?

STAINES: The ideas of the age, the revolution in France, the passing years have developed a wealth of sympathy for the men, antipathy for Bligh, and elevated Fletcher Christian to lion.

CHRISTIAN: Lion?

STAINES: That's the pamphlets, the chop houses and the people.

PIPON: Not the Admiralty.

CHRISTIAN: They'd hang Christian if he were alive?

PIPON: They would.

CHRISTIAN: There's one of the women Te Lahu would like to go back to Tahiti, she has children there, and never had none here.

STAINES: Certainly.

CHRISTIAN: I will stay. Til death. My family is here. And, as you can see, the Lord has a full slate of work for me.

THE END.